OUR DEBT TO ANTIQUITY

OUR DEBT TO ANTIQUITY

BY

PROFESSOR ZIELINSKI

TRANSLATED, WITH INTRODUCTION AND NOTES, BY

PROFESSOR H. A. STRONG, LL.D.

AND

HUGH STEWART, B.A.

KENNIKAT PRESS
Port Washington, N. Y./London

OUR DEBT TO ANTIQUITY

First published in 1909
Reissued in 1971 by Kennikat Press
Library of Congress Catalog Card No: 75-113317
ISBN 0-8046-1205-6

Manufactured by Taylor Publishing Company Dallas, Texas

KENNIKAT CLASSICS SERIES

INTRODUCTION

THE following lectures were delivered by Professor Zielinski of St. Petersburg University in the spring of 1903 to the highest classes of the secondary schools in the capital. In the same year they were published in the Journal of the Ministry for Popular Education and appeared in separate book form. Despite a somewhat unfavourable reception in the Press the work created widespread interest, and a second edition was soon called for. In preparing it Professor Zielinski retained the form of the first. "I do not want to undo it and undo therewith the memory of hours which I count among the happiest in my life." But he emphasises the fact that this second edition, which the translators have used, is meant for the world at large. He feels strongly and reasonably that "the regeneration of the classical school, which is indispensable in the interests of Russian culture, will come about only when Society itself is convinced of its necessity."

It is hoped that the work may be found of no less interest to English readers than it has proved to students on the Continent. Its interest seems to the translators to consist first and foremost in the reasons advanced for the maintenance of the classics as the groundwork of education. These arguments are in some cases different from those which we are accustomed to hear from partisans of the classical school in Western Europe. The whole question indeed is surveyed from a fresh standpoint; the lectures form a stimulating and suggestive treatment of a familiar subject on new lines. Certain statements and theories are perhaps open to question, but the work throughout is distinguished by a high level of discussion, unflagging spirits, and a philosophic breadth of view which make powerful and constant claims on the reader's interest and sympathy. A welcome note of enthusiasm and insight pervades the whole subject, and the clear-sighted and original ideas that are strewn throughout the pages must arrest the attention and compel thought. They are for the most part expressed with that characteristically Russian naïveté and use of vigorous and illuminating similes which give the style a flavour of the peculiar charm familiar to readers of Russian literature.

It will in addition be of interest to English readers to note the importance attached to the study of Latin by a teacher in a country which looks back to Byzantine Greek as its classical language. This judgment is in remarkable contrast with the view which obtains generally among the professor's countrymen, and is based on the small part played by Rome in Russian civilisation. The history of classical study in Russia is more in accordance with this latter view, although it cannot be said to have advanced the cause of Greek. The record is one of constant vicissitudes, but not at any time of prosperity. In archæology, indeed, a great deal of good work has been done, the importance of which has not yet been grasped by Western students, but classical scholarship generally has been but a feeble and languishing product. At the present day, beyond a few notable exceptions, among whom Professor Zielinski himself is a prominent figure, it is at a low ebb indeed, if that term be permissible in a case where the tides were never high. The small group of leaders might take their place in the van of European scholarship, but the unenthusiastic rank and file lag far behind. In most of the gymnasia Greek is not taught at all, and the standard of Latin required for the "Attestat Zrailosti," the "certificate of maturity," which corresponds in a sense with our "Leaving Certificate" (cf. note on page 207), is undoubtedly low. With these facts borne in mind Professor Zielinski's triumphant vindication of his cause gains a new significance.

Scholars in our own country would probably have dwelt on some other considerations in favour of classical study besides those mentioned by the Russian lecturer. One of these might well have been that the characters and the social life described in the classics are simple and easy of comprehension, and as such afford useful models to the students of a mature and complicated civilisation. But it is to be hoped that those who come forward to champion the cause of classical studies will insist more and more that Latin should be learnt in connection with French and, if possible, the other Romance languages. The teacher of Latin should be a good French scholar and should possess an adequate knowledge of French in its several stages. Conversely the French teacher should be a good Latinist. If French and Latin were taught as thus intimately connected, the pupil would develop an intuitive instinct of the evolutionary nature of language in general, and would acquire from a knowledge of the different features in French a similar instinct for the processes of Comparative Philology. For it should be noted that the various processes which take place in language such as sound change, change of meaning, contamination, and so forth, may be instanced from the history of Latin and French; and it is surely wiser to illustrate one known language by another than to compare a known language with an unknown one, such as Latin with Sanskrit or Slavonic.

The German translation of Professor Zielinski's lectures is by Herr E. Schoeler. Herr Weicher, of the Dieterich'sche Verlagsbuchhandlung, Leipzig, most kindly allowed us to compare the German translation with our own.

ANALYTICAL TABLE OF CONTENTS

LECTURE I

LECTURE II

LECTURE III

LECTURE IV

LECTURE VI

LECTURE VII

LECTURE VIII

OUR DEBT TO ANTIQUITY

LECTURE I

THE task before me is to interpret to my hearers, as far as the time at our disposal and my powers permit, the importance of the special department of knowledge of which I am the accredited representative at the St. Petersburg University: a department which I may briefly indicate by the title "Antiquity." Our end may be gained by three different ways, corresponding to the threefold aspect of the subject itself. Antiquity forms, in the first place, the subject-matter of that science which is commonly, though in some respects erroneously, called "Classical Philology"; in the second place, it contributes an element to the intellectual and moral culture of modern European society; in the third place—and here its significance especially touches you, my hearers—it forms one of the subjects taught in the "Privileged" secondary schools of Russia—the so-called Classical Gymnasia.

Each of these points of view reveals to us a new aspect of Antiquity: each compels the trained scholar to range himself in direct opposition to the opinion prevalent to-day among the educated in every country, and particularly in Russia. Men, indeed, have made up their minds that what is called "Classical Philology" is a science which, however zealously cultivated, yet affords no longer any interesting problems for our solution. Our expert, however, will tell you that never has it had such interest for us as to-day: that the entire work of previous generations was merely preparatory—in fact, was merely the foundation on which we are only now beginning to raise the actual structure of our knowledge; that problems ever new, challenging research and demanding solution, meet us at every step in the field of our progress.

Again, in regard to the element contributed by Antiquity to modern culture, a belief rules abroad that Antiquity plays a meaningless part in the world of to-day; that it has no significance for modern culture; and that it has long since been superseded by the achievements of modern thought. But our expert, again, will assure us that our modern culture, both intellectual and moral, has never been so closely bound up with Antiquity as to-day, and has never stood in such pressing need of its contributions. He will tell us, further, that we have never been so well equipped for understanding and assimilating it as to-day. Finally, in regard to Antiquity as an element of education, people are disposed to deem it merely a singular survival, which has maintained its footing in our modern school curriculum in some unintelligible way and for some unintelligible reason, but which is destined to make a speedy and final disappearance. But the man who understands the true position of affairs will rejoin that Antiquity, from its very nature and essence, owing to both historical and psychological causes, is and must be considered an organic element of education in European schools, and that if it be destined to disappear entirely its end will coincide with the end of modern European culture.

We have, then, these three antitheses; and you will agree that sharper cannot easily be formulated. I am afraid that the very statement of these antitheses may trouble you and dispose you to look with suspicion on what I have to say. And as such an *à priori* prejudice may conceivably weaken the effect of the lecturer's words on the minds of his audience, pray allow me to dispel it, as far as prejudice can be dispelled by the operation of reason. Indeed, I can imagine your objection to be stated thus broadly: "Does not the mere composition of the two parties to the dispute show who is right and who is wrong? Is it possible that the vast majority of men should be wrong, and that the expert of whom you speak, and with whom you probably identify yourself, Professor, should be right?

"Let us leave 'Classical Philology' out of account for the moment: it has no interest for the world at large, so the world at large has the right to ignore it; but Antiquity as an element in culture, Antiquity as a vital factor in education—can we really admit that men have gone so far astray in settling questions which touch them so nearly? 'Vox populi, vox Dei' is no mere idle saying." Here I could make a reservation, and a fairly important one, with respect to this majority of which we hear so much; but let that pass. Let it be even as you say. Still, I cannot admit the applicability of the proverb about the *vox populi* to this majority, whether it be found to exist in reality or in imagination only: the history of all ages protests loudly against such an application. Only reflect how Rome drove the early Christians into the arena; think how Spain raged against the heretics, or Germany against the witches; think of the unanimous support long afforded to institutions like negro slavery in America, or serfdom in Russia, and you will agree that the "vox populi" is in truth only too often the *vox Diaboli*, and not the *vox Dei*. To-day we not only condemn such manifestations of the popular will: we explain them dispassionately; that is no bad thing. We show the reasons which in all the cases I have indicated have forced men to conclusions so adverse to their true interests. And in the present case also we can adopt the same attitude; in the present case also we can—and an attempt to do so will, if time permit, form part of my last lecture—analyse the cause of the adverse position taken up by modern critics against Antiquity. We can distinguish the part played therein by well-intentioned and involuntary delusion from that which we must ascribe to intentional deception. For the moment my purpose is different: I am anxious only to shatter your simple faith—if you have a faith—in the infallibility of public opinion, and to protest against the misapplication of the proverb "Vox populi, vox Dei."

The proper meaning of this saying I will proceed to explain to you. Where must we look to hear the voice of God? Not in the deafening clamour which is so often the expression of mere passionate excitement, but in the calm, dispassionate command of that mysterious will which points out to Humanity the path of development in Civilisation. In remote ages, before mankind had any inkling of the physiology of digestion or of Organic Chemistry, that voice warned mankind that if it would attain the highest possible degree of perfection, it should select as its main article of diet—*Bread*. The Greeks, who could feel wonder for what really merited that emotion, recognised rightly enough the divine nature of this voice; they believed it to be the voice of their goddess Dêmêter. The Biology of the present day, which does not recognise Metaphysics, or which, to speak more correctly, has introduced, instead of the honoured Theological Metaphysics of former times, its own special scheme of Biological Metaphysics, sees in that voice the effect of the Law of Natural Selection which it itself discovered, a law entirely analogous to that which has assigned its own proper diet to every living animal. Yes, gentlemen, this Law of Natural Selection which, in cases where Human Society is its subject, bears the title of "Sociological Selection"—that is the real *vox populi* and *vox Dei*.

Let us now ask, in what relation does this Law stand to our present question? the question as to the part played by Antiquity in the education imparted to the youth of our day, or, more briefly, to classical education. This, then, is the relation: now, nearly fifteen hundred years after the fall of Rome, and more than two thousand years after the fall of Greece, we find ourselves disputing as to whether the languages spoken by the two classical nations of Antiquity shall, or shall not, occupy the central place in the teaching of our schools. You must needs concede to me, gentlemen, that the unanimous testimony of centuries is a far more impressive fact than the ephemeral verdict of modern society, even were its unanimity less fictitious than in fact it is. Think of the picture which the Neva presents when the fatal south-west wind is blowing! The set of its waves is plainly to the east. The river seems running upstream into the lake of Ladoga. And yet you know that every drop of that lake, thanks to an invisible but very real fall in the earth's surface, is making its way into the Gulf of Finland; and that the only result of this upstream current produced by the wind is a temporary overflow of the Galeerenhafen. The same phenomenon is to be witnessed in a community and in public opinion. In them, as in our Neva, there are not one, but two currents. There is one which is for show—noisy, tumultuous, and capricious, and followed by inundations and misfortunes of every kind; the other, whose very existence is hardly suspected by the former, is quiet, soundless, and irresistible. Two currents, or, if you like, two souls, two "I's." You may adopt for society as a whole the sharp division which Fr. Nietzsche has wittily proposed for the individual members which compose it. He contrasts the "little I," which is self-conscious and carries, relatively speaking, but small weight, with the "great I," which, though sub-conscious, still prescribes with sovereign power the course of public progress. Well, this unfavourable view entertained by the contemporary world as to a training in the classics, a view which you may be inclined to oppose to my apparently isolated opinion, is the product, not of the modern world in its entirety, but merely of its *little I*. Of course, this "little I" can, and actually does, inflict on me as an individual a certain amount of annoyance; but it has no weight with me as a thinking man and an historian. As such I am in duty bound to attend not to its voice, but to the voice of the mysterious "great I" which directs its destiny. And there I hear something quite different; the "little I" of the modern world repeats in all the notes of the scale: "Down with classical training!" The "greater I," however, says to us: "Cherish it as the apple of your eye!" Or, to speak more correctly, it does not actually say this to us; it has itself cherished classical education for some fifteen or twenty centuries, disregarding the repeated protests of its own "little I"; and you may be sure that it will cherish it in the future as in the past.

However, we have arrived at this result in favour of Antiquity only incidentally. In our next remarks we must seek to establish our claims with more detailed arguments. Do not attach, for the meantime, any importance to our present result, and merely bear in mind what I have said about the two currents of public opinion and their relative value. And now let us approach the subject.

At the beginning of my lecture I insisted on the threefold significance of Antiquity for us: purely scientific, cultural, and educational. We will, however, adopt another order in our course; we will begin with what concerns you all, and conclude with what directly affects, or rather will affect, but a few among you.

And so, wherein lies the educational importance of a study of Antiquity?

Assuming, first of all, that my answer to this question must be a confession of ignorance, or that it prove in any other way unsatisfactory, what would follow? When I explained to you just now the purport of the Law of Sociological Selection, I referred you, as an illustration of my meaning, to one remarkable result of such selection, whereby bread has come to be the principal article of diet of civilised man. Permit me now to use this illustration for a picture or allegory, which, indeed, has served me once before in a similar case. Suppose that in the times when men were inclined to regard the human organism as a mechanism, in the days of Helvétius* and La Mettrie,† a commission had been appointed to reform the diet of mankind. The speeches of the opponents of the traditional methods of diet would have first and foremost drawn a gloomy picture of the physical condition of mankind at that period. Man lives some sixty or seventy years at most, though Nature intended him to live two hundred years—this was precisely the opinion, later on, of Hufeland‡—and pray what sort of a life has he during the brief space of his existence? He is feeble and clumsy; he ages rapidly; and think of all the failures of physical life! etc.

Whence all this misery? Simply because his diet is irrational. Diet ought to renew the human body; but our diet consists mainly of materials which the human body does not require and, indeed, rids itself of anew, as entirely useless. Our bodies need flesh, blood, muscles, marrow, etc. In spite of this demand, we supply them almost entirely with a vegetarian diet, of which bread forms the main factor. The mischief caused by bread is that it stands completely in the way of other articles of diet which are really useful; to prove its worthlessness you need only

* Claude Adrien Helvétius (1715–71), author of "De l'Esprit et de l'Homme."

† Julien Offray de la Mettrie (1709–51), author of "Histoire Naturelle de l'Ame": "Homme Machine": "Homme Plante": "Discours sur le Bonheur": "L'Art de Jouir," etc.

‡ C. W. Hufeland (1762–1836), author of "Makrobiotik."

consider the human body. Are our arms, legs, hands, and lungs composed of dough? Certainly not. Of what, then? Of blood, flesh, muscle, bones, and so on. Well, then, pray give us a genuinely satisfying diet, answering to the composition of our bodies; give us a uniform diet to nourish the body generally, containing in one harmonious, evenly-proportioned compound every element needed by us for the renovation of our physical nature—flesh, blood, bones, muscles, and so on. Then, and not till then, will the failures of physical life disappear; then a man will live a couple of centuries, and his youth will endure longer than his life to-day, and so on. Now, what might a supporter of the traditional diet have urged by way of rejoinder? What might have been his reply when challenged to prove the value of bread as nourishment?

At the present day, of course, an answer suggests itself as possible which explains quite satisfactorily all the difficulties; on the one hand, Physiology has thrown a light on the process of digestion in all its details; on the other, Organic Chemistry has analysed our diet to its component parts. Chemistry warrants us in asserting that bread contains all, or nearly all, the constituents of food necessary for the human body; Physiology helps us to trace the way by which our organism assimilates these materials. But we were supposing ourselves in a period when the process of digestion was but very imperfectly understood, while Organic Chemistry was quite unknown ; and so, I repeat, what could the supporters of the traditional methods of diet reply to the champions of empirical dietetics of those days ? I fancy their reply might have been as follows : "You ask in what the dietetic value of bread, and, generally speaking, of a vegetable diet, consists. That I cannot tell you. But the fact remains that the nations which have adopted our food system are therewith the bearers of civilisation, while those which diet themselves according to your theories are only the very rudest of barbarians. It is also true that the civilised nations multiply and spread, while the savages who feed on a meat diet are decreasing in number and are being pushed ever further into the background. Further, it is a fact that civilised man, when he is by the force of circumstances constrained to deny himself the use of bread and fruit, and to adopt exclusively a meat diet, becomes enfeebled and dies out. Finally, it is a fact that you yourselves, while you have correctly pointed out the shortcomings of our physical life, have still failed to prove that those shortcomings are the natural result of our system of diet ; nor have you deigned to bestow any notice on the circumstance that those who follow your system are neither longer lived, nor stronger, nor handsomer, nor healthier than we ; which seems a mere mockery of the empirical method."

Such, I fancy, would have been the answer of a supporter of the traditional dietetic system, and his inference would have been unassailable. Now

I pass on to our present question. You ask me to show you wherein lies the educational value of Antiquity. I preface my answer by a question, namely: "Has Psychology clearly defined and explained the process of intellectual digestion in all its details? Does there exist a system of Organic Chemistry applicable to intellectual diet and capable of providing a qualitative and quantitative analysis of this diet?" Should you then admit that the sciences which I have in view are sciences of the future, known to us at present only in their beginnings, you authorise me thereby to make this rejoinder: "What is the educational value of the study of Antiquity? That I do not, indeed, know; but it is a fact that the system of classical education dates from time out of mind; that it has at the present day spread to all the nations who enjoy the benefit of so-called European civilisation, and who, indeed, could not be called civilised till they adopted this system. It is, further, true that if we were to follow the methods of the meteorologists and express the vicissitudes which the system of classical education has experienced in the different countries where it has been adopted throughout all the period of their existence by the figure of a curve, this curve would be found to express at the same time the variations in the intellectual culture of these same nations. It would thus demonstrate the close dependence of the general culture of any given country on the degree of importance attached to classical education.

Thirdly, it is a fact that in the present day also the intellectual influence of any given nation asserts itself in proportion as classical education prevails in its schools; whereas nations who discard this system—the Spaniards, for instance—play no great part in the world of ideas, in spite of their large population and glorious past. It is also true that in Russia the blow inflicted on classical education by the reform of the Gymnasia in the year 1890 has entailed a general depression of the level of education on the young men who leave our Gymnasia, as is admitted even by our opponents. And, lastly, it is true that those who depict the shortcomings of our Gymnasia in such sombre colours have failed to show that these shortcomings are the result of classical education; they obstinately refuse to consider the fact that the same shortcomings are manifest in the pupils of the secondary schools in which classical education plays no part."

The inference is unassailable. In the interests of the mental culture of the Russian people we are bound to aim at the highest possible level of classical training in our Gymnasia, regardless as to whether we succeed or not in giving a satisfactory answer to the question respecting the educational value of a study of Antiquity.

And now, before proceeding further, let us look back a little. A consideration of the history of culture led us to the conclusion that the study of the Classics offers in itself the standard of intellectual diet of the rising generation. I asserted that this conclusion was unassailable; and, in truth, every one who is accustomed to weigh his words and subordinate his feelings to his reason in matters of Science—and it is with such that we have now to deal—is bound to agree with me. But, unfortunately, such persons are rare. Ordinary people subordinate their reason to their feelings; when any proposition which they dislike is proved to them to be true, they try to find in what you say some handle for contradiction; and if they succeed in hitting on any rejoinder which has but an external resemblance to a logical argument, they then allege, and often themselves actually believe, that they have refuted you. Of course, it is quite impossible to foresee refutations of this nature. One way, and one alone, leads to truth; whereas the paths to error are manifold. But as I am acquainted with much of what has been written on the question of the secondary schools, I can imagine that my adversaries will find two "handles" in my statements.

This is the first one. I have just said, "in the interests of the mental culture of the Russian people." I took it for granted that any conclusions which might be drawn from the fluctuations of culture in Europe generally must be equally applicable to Russia. Is this assumption correct? In the ranks of my opponents there are not a few who will refuse to recognise this connection. "No," say they, "the claims of a classical education are not supported by the history of Russia." On this plea they discard classical education, and then proceed to launch projects of a special school curriculum of their own, forgetting, however, to enquire whether its claims are supported by the history of Russia or not. Matters, in truth, stand thus. However scanty the support given to the claims of a classical education by the facts of Russian history, any other type of education, existing or proposed, finds in them absolutely no support. But for us this is not by any means the principal consideration. The main point is this: Russia for a long time possessed no system of classical education; the result was that during all that period it was not an educated nation; nor did it become so till the introduction of classics as an educational medium. That is a fact, and, moreover, one which fully confirms my conclusions.

The second objection runs parallel to the first and stands in the same relation to it as time to space. Our opponents in this camp endeavour to assume for modern times just such another exceptional position as their allies assumed for Russia. "In old times," say they, "the study of Antiquity really formed an important branch of learning, for it had lessons to teach; but at the present day we have travelled far beyond it, and we have nothing more to learn from it." These opponents are very easily refuted; we have merely to confront them with the question: "When do they believe that we outstripped Antiquity?" That question they cannot answer. The matter really stands thus. The question of classical education, as we have seen, is subject to the law of Sociological Selection. The operation of this law is determined by what is known as the " Heterogeneity of purposes " ; that is to say, the non-correspondence of the real and unconscious purpose with the apparent and conscious purpose. Thus the apparent purpose of which the bee is conscious when it is enticed into the recesses of a flower is that the creature may enjoy the sweet juice ; the real purpose, on the other hand, of which the bee is unconscious, is that the stamina of the flower should be pulled about and thereby produce its fructification.

Precisely the same thing happens in this case also. The real purpose of Sociological Selection —it will be understood, of course, that I employ the word " purpose " here in the relative sense in which it is generally used in modern Biology— in its maintenance of classical education has been at all times one and the same—namely, the intellectual and moral improvement of humanity. But the apparent purposes of which the world was conscious were different. They varied at different times ; and this leads us to make two interesting observations. In the first place, scarcely has one of these apparent purposes served its time, so to say, when another steps forward to take its place. Secondly, those nations which mistook the ostensible apparent purpose for the real one and who endeavoured to achieve it, not by the path which the law of selection indicated to them, but by a shorter and more convenient path, have had a hard judgment pronounced on them for their would-be omniscience by the tribunal of history. This is precisely what we see in biology and biological laws.

Originally, in the early Middle Ages, the apparent purpose of classical education was the understanding of Holy Scripture and of the Liturgy, the works of the Church Fathers, the lives of the saints, and so on. Of course, there was another method, more simple and convenient for attaining this end, namely, the translation of all these writings into the mother tongue. This method was adopted by the nations of the Christian East, and the consequence was that the advance of culture left those nations hopelessly behind. At a later period, in the second half of the Middle Ages, this purpose retired to the background in favour of another—a knowledge of ancient science, as expounded, of course, in the classical languages. Here, also, another shorter and more convenient road was at the service of those who wished it—namely, the translation of the scientific works of the Ancients into the mother tongue. This was the course adopted by the Arabs, and it brought Mahommedan civilisation, after a brief period of prosperity, to a speedy and irretrievable ruin; as, indeed, was quite natural, since the Arabs transplanted on to their own ground merely the flowers of Antiquity severed from their roots, the ancient languages.

But this plan, too, was discarded at the end of the Middle Ages; modern Europe had no sooner assimilated the science of the ancients than it passed beyond it. . . . To the question, then, propounded above—namely, When did we outstrip Antiquity in the sphere of science? our reply must be: To some extent as early as the Middle Ages. That period discovered Sciences that were unknown or almost unknown to the ancients, as, for example, Algebra, Trigonometry, Chemistry, and so on, and raised the Sciences already known to a higher degree. It now seemed that Antiquity might really be dispensed with, and classical culture did indeed begin to decline in the fourteenth century. But precisely in this century this same culture bloomed afresh, rapidly and brilliantly; the Renaissance has begun. Ancient art, not merely figurative, such as architecture, sculpture, painting, but oratorical also, was discovered anew. Men began to study the Latin language for the sake of its beauties in respect to form, and to reproduce them both in prose and verse. This is what is known as the Old Humanistic movement. The Latin language became once again the educator, so to say, of the languages of modern Europe. The result of this influence of Latin is seen in the elasticity and strength, in the artistic technique, of modern prose and poetry. The result, then, was attained, and it seemed that Antiquity might now be relegated to archæological shelves. But no! Scarcely had this purpose begun to recede into the background when a fresh plan, the fourth of these transitory purposes, appeared to take its place. The intellectual value of ancient literature was discovered, Philosophy being its crown and consummation. Before that time men had learnt Latin to be able to speak well and write well; now they learnt it to be able to think well and judge well, *pour bien raisonner.*

Such was the *mot d'ordre* of the so-called "enlightened views" which started in England during the seventeenth century and which continued in France during the eighteenth century and were reflected in the culture of the rest of the Europe of that time: the time of Newton, Voltaire, Frederick the Great, and Catherine. But already, in the eighteenth century, this one-sided intellectualism called forth a reaction which began in England and in France (as instanced by Rousseau), but attained special force in the Germany of Winkelmann and Goethe. The watchword was now the harmonious development of mankind in the way pointed out by Nature, and the true method of attaining this ideal was seen to be once again—the study of Antiquity.

Accordingly, the Gymnasia set about their new task with extreme energy. This is the so-called "New Humanistic" movement. Then, for the first time, the Greek language and literature claimed equal rights with the Latin, for the leaders of thought of that day believed quite rightly that the life of Greece approached their ideal nearer than the life of Rome. At the present moment we are again in a period of transition, and we see already clearly traced the new point of view from which the coming century will regard Antiquity. The development of the Natural

Sciences has given prominence to the principle of Evolution: Antiquity has become doubly precious to us as the cradle of every one of the ideas which we have hitherto cherished. And we see how Humanism finds itself at variance with the so-called Historic movement in the very questions connected with classical education. It seems, moreover, that the latter school is gaining the day. Of course, we shall have to return to this extremely important consideration. For the present, however, it will be sufficient to assure you that this is already the sixth conscious attitude in regard to the importance of the study of Antiquity. It has made its appearance just in the nick of time to relieve the New Humanistic attitude.

It is curious, too, to trace the changes which have passed over the methods of instruction in classical education according to the different points of view from which the purpose of this study was apprehended. I am unable to dwell on this at length. I must rest content with indicating the most obvious and palpable changes which are expressed in the choice of authors at each different epoch. During the first period, when Latin was studied for the salvation of the soul, we find, as is natural, that religious works form the central point of the curriculum. During the second, which we may call the scientific period, the main subjects of study were the handbooks of the respective sciences, such as the Latin Aristotle and the so-called *Artes*; that is to say, treatises on Mathematics and Astronomy, and also on Medicine and Law, and so on. In the third, or Old Humanist epoch, it was Cicero as the master of Latin oratory. In the fourth, the epoch of "enlightenment," it was Cicero again, but this time as the philosopher. In the fifth, the New Humanistic period, it was Homer, the tragic poets, and Horace. We are living on the traditions of this period, but already there is felt a growing need of a careful selection from ancient literature, so as to represent Antiquity to young scholars as precisely the cradle of our ideas.

Quite recently Wilamowitz in Germany has sought to meet this need by compiling a Greek "Reading Book," and his experiment has deeply interested all the teaching profession in his own country. No doubt this movement will in time reach us in Russia as well; very probably it would have made its presence felt already, were it not for the recent unrest in our schools. However this may be, I have shown you the series of changing points of view from which the study of Antiquity has been regarded during the different periods of our civilisation. This, too, may serve as an answer to the ignorant reproach that we have nothing now to learn from Antiquity, as we have outstripped it; and likewise to the equally ignorant reproach that classical studies have come to a standstill and are not keeping up with the times. But all these aims were, as I have stated, transitory. They were aims towards which society consciously strove in each of the periods mentioned, and society has rendered an account for them alike to itself and to us. The true aim, however, of which men were not conscious, was the all-important goal to which all selection tends —namely, the improvement of Humanity: in this case man's cultural, that is to say, his intellectual and moral improvement.

But, it may be asked, in what way does the path of classical education tend to improve mankind intellectually and morally? This very question suggests another, Wherein lies the educational value of Antiquity? We have already raised this latter question, and before answering it I proved to you that, whether our answer may seem satisfactory or not, the fact remains indisputable that the study of Antiquity is an extremely important element in education. This has been unmistakably shown, quite independently of that answer, by considerations adduced from the history of culture. I beg you to bear in mind this fact: I attach the greatest importance to it. Precisely in the same way the value of bread as an article of diet was well established long before it had been proved by Physiology and Organic Chemistry. What is Physiology in this instance? The analysis of the consuming organism. And Chemistry? The analysis of the substance consumed. Now substitute mind for body, education for diet, and Antiquity for bread. Do there, then, exist sciences in this connection analogous to Physiology and Organic Chemistry? that is to say, sciences which teach us how to analyse the organism of the consumer and the matter consumed? Let us see.

The consuming element is in this case the human intellect. Its analysis is the business of Psychology, and that science is at present still in a state of infancy. Psychology is as yet unable to reply to all the questions addressed to her. This is, indeed, true of Physiology as well; but still, the latter science has been vastly more developed, and is older alike in years and in experience. Now, as to the analysis of the diet for consumption, that is to say, Antiquity. This analysis is not intrinsically very difficult, but in this case a study of the effects of its elements upon man's psychological nature is indispensable; in fact, a kind of *psychological science of knowledges*. And no such science is yet in existence, as the mere combination of the words shows you. So, gentlemen, you must not ask too much from me. I have promised you to answer the question proposed, and will do so as far as possible with the present state of *Psychological* sciences. As I have remarked, these are sciences of the Future; yet they have already established certain principles upon a fairly sure basis, and their methods are becoming ever more and more accurate, so that we are at least able to apprehend in what manner and in what direction a satisfactory answer to the questions which beset us is to be looked for. Yes, I can affirm so much; but I beg you to remember that this is merely a temporary answer, and that a much fuller and more convincing answer can be given only by our posterity. But before fulfilling my promise I must beg you to bear with me while I make a few remarks on the real meaning of the term "educational value." I am particularly anxious that you should accept nothing from me without a severe custom-house scrutiny, so to speak. This may detain us for a few minutes, but in return I shall hope to gain later on somewhat more of your confidence.

And so I put the question: In what sense are we to understand the expression "educational value"?

Let us begin with the most concrete example possible. A carpenter has a son. He wishes to teach him a carpenter's trade. In this instance the problem is simple and intelligible to all. The carpenter's schooling prepares the boy directly for real life; every knack of the trade which the boy learns will be eminently useful to him in his future work, and in precisely the same way. We can easily picture to ourselves a carpenter's school; it will be, in fact, what we call a professional or technical school. Is there any justification for its existence? Undoubtedly there is, if you admit that it is possible or desirable to settle the trade or profession of a boy at such an early age. But is the principle of "professional utilitarianism" applicable to intellectual as well as to manual training? To some extent this may be so, as theological schools, military and naval academies, and other secondary schools of the kind may serve to show; but it is only partially applicable.

For most intellectual professions there are no such schools in existence; and even those which I have just mentioned are trying more and more to free themselves from their narrow professional character and to look with favour on a general education at the expense of any special branch. And, generally speaking, it is recognised that we need schools which do not insist upon determining *à priori* the future profession of their scholars.

What, then, should be the nature of such schools, assuming always that they are intended to prepare their scholars for real life, that is to say, for their future trade or profession? This is the problem of squaring the circle as applied to educational questions; and the efforts made to-day to solve it are as successful as those directed in former days at the solution of that famous mathematical puzzle itself. I will indicate certain methods of solving the problem which recommend themselves to the man in the street. The first of these is as follows:

There is a demand for a school to train the future lawyers, doctors, professors of Natural History, engineers, mathematicians, scholars, and so on; so far, so good. Its programme will embrace all the subjects of study which are common to all these departments of science. The shortcomings of this system are plain enough; the fact is that there are no such common courses of study, or, at least, extremely few. You have only to compare the lists of lectures provided for the

Faculty of Law with those for the Faculty of Natural Science, or the programme of courses in history and classics with that of any technical institute, and you will be convinced of this. Now consider the second possible way. Select, if you please, in equal proportions courses of Law, Medicine, Physics, Mathematics, History, Classics, and other subjects, and out of these try and concoct a programme fit for a secondary school! Now, there are people simple enough to believe that this is feasible; it is, however, an utter impossibility. In the first place we are confronted with a confusing and deadening multiplicity of subjects, and in the second place the principle of utilitarianism is not even now maintained, for such a school cannot offer any of its scholars more than a tenth part of what he requires. Thus we may ask, what sort of a school is that which combines a bare tenth of useful material with nine-tenths of ballast?

There is a third way. Admitting the untenability of the first two solutions, one may propose to disregard entirely in our secondary schools the future career of our scholars, and demand merely that they leave the schools as educated persons. In other words, professional and utilitarian considerations are deliberately eschewed and the principle merely of education introduced. So far, so good. But what do we mean by an educated person? The answer cannot be far to seek; for we know that there are educated persons. What, then, must one know to be an educated person?

An author of great reputation in educational matters has proposed a radical measure for the solution of this problem. His idea was to subject educated persons to a catechism, in other words, to an examination, and so establish a standard of departments of knowledge without which a man would not be "educated," and then to make these departments of knowledge the subjects of school-instruction. It would be amusing to carry out this plan and watch the results. You understand, of course, that under this system those departments of knowledge which one educated man possesses still do not fall into the general programme if there be a second educated man who does not possess them, for that shows that one can be educated even without their possession. Indeed, we might imagine a prodigy who could tell us the names of thirty Patagonian villages—that is his speciality; but we could incorporate into our programme only what all educated society, or at least the greater part of it, knows about Patagonia; that is to say, nothing at all. And so it would be with all the other courses. And the net result would be: in Arithmetic the four rules concerning whole numbers, with a general knowledge of fractions; in Geometry, a few ordinary ideas about figures and solid bodies; in Algebra, nothing; in Trigonometry, nothing; and so on in its entirety; a programme which one or two Gymnasium classes would fully exhaust. It is easy to see that this way, too, fails to lead us to our goal. What, then, is the mistake? It lies in this, that we consider education to be the mere acquirement of knowledge. But whereas knowledge is forgotten, education is never lost; an educated person, even though he have forgotten all that he has learnt, remains an educated person. In making this statement I am very far from wishing to under-estimate the importance of knowledge; on the contrary, I maintain that a man's utility is in proportion to his knowledge. But, gentlemen, different persons require different branches of knowledge. That is the case even at present, and will in the future be more the case than ever; for knowledge is ever becoming more and more specialised. The number of branches of knowledge indispensable to all, or indeed to all educated persons, is even at present far from large, and must diminish in every generation as knowledge itself continues to increase and consequently to be specialised. And thus to draw up the courses of learning for our secondary schools on these principles is an impossibility. And still it is the duty of such schools to give all those who are afterwards to be educated persons precisely what is likely to benefit them all alike; that is their whole object. And how shall they best fulfil this duty? Obviously by preparing a scholar's mind to embrace any branch of knowledge which he may need afterwards with the least possible expenditure of time and strength, and with the greatest possible advantage to himself. This is a truism, stale if you will, but a truism that defies contradiction and is, in fact, irrefutable.

If it were my task to draw up a programme for our secondary schools, I would endeavour to convince you, on the grounds of what I have said, that it must contain the following: firstly, courses providing a general knowledge, and secondly, courses providing a general education; the latter class would naturally rank as the more important. And to this latter class would naturally belong the courses on Mathematics, Physics, and Classics, corresponding to the three methods of human thought—the deductive, the inductive-experimental, and the inductive-observant. But, as I remarked at the beginning of the lecture, my task is a narrower one. I intend to speak of the educational value only of my own course; that is to say, the Study of Antiquity.

I must, by the way, in this place take steps to prevent your casting on me a greater responsibility than I am willing and able to bear. I know that many speakers and writers are continually proving to you that the time which you have expended on the study of the ancient classics is so much time lost to no purpose whatever, and that you are wont to applaud this statement. I mean, however, to prove to you, gentlemen, that you have not wasted your time, though I run the risk of saying what may displease you. But, gentlemen, that one risk is enough for me. I will not accept responsibility for the series of ideas and feelings which you possibly connect with the idea of "classicism" and a "classical school." I am painfully aware that our classical school has many shortcomings: some more, some less serious, as depending on the qualifications of the teachers and the pupils; and, indeed, this factor is of more importance than all the programmes and circulars in the world. But I know, too, that because Hygiene is on a bad footing in Turkey it does not follow that the science of medicine has proved useless everywhere. Thus my task does not consist in praising the merits of this or that gymnasium, but, as I said, in putting clearly before you the advantages of a study of Antiquity, pursued according to methods which meet with my approval, and which a long experience has taught me to be possible as well.

I shall now proceed to the solution of that problem. What I have said hitherto has been solely with the object of explaining its meaning and of clearing away the ground. It may be that I have devoted too much time to this purpose and have set too little store by your attention, observation, and impartial judgment. If this be so, I beg you to excuse me. I have been schooled by bitter experiences, for which, too, I am obliged to people in whom I had far more reason to expect all these virtues than in yourselves.

LECTURE II *

THE ancient world—as the term itself shows—covers an extremely wide, rich, and many-sided department of knowledge. It is, indeed, a peculiar "World," sharply marked off from our own, but still connected with it by a thousand links, of most of which we are unconscious. The study of this world, and the utilising of its ideas for the enrichment of the intellectual and moral culture of the present world—and the former aim is useless without the latter—that is the enviable task of the band of scholars to whom I have the honour and the good fortune to belong. The pupils in our secondary schools get to know this world of Antiquity only to a very small degree, by mastering the mere elements of classical learning, which enter into the programme of so-called classical education. These elements are, first, the scheme of both classical languages in their

* The word *apperception* is here used in the sense in which it was employed by Herbart, to denote the process which affects progressively a series of mental states, each such state acquiring during the orderly progression of such series a new set of facts or determinations which modify or alter the primary state. Thus a subject learnt by apperception entails a regular and orderly advance of knowledge, the new facts or impressions acquired modifying, or it may be fundamentally changing, the state of mind resulting from previous experiences.

tripartite division: Etymology, Semasiology (vulgo Vocabulary), and Syntax; in the second place, selections chosen from the best productions of ancient literature, which are read and explained in the original; thirdly, such acquaintance with the various aspects of Antiquity as is promoted by a journey through ancient history, by the perusal of isolated passages in translations, by stories of ancient life, by brief introductory lectures to ancient philosophy, literature, civil and criminal law, by dissertations on monuments of ancient art, by the information contained in good modern novels dealing with the life of the ancients, and, wherever possible, by a cursory perusal of entire "family and domestic" works, and so on.

These three elements of classical learning must form our starting-point, or rather the two first named; the third must wait for discussion till the second part of my lectures, which is devoted to the value of Antiquity for modern culture. And so to begin with the first: Wherein consists the educational value of the ancient languages as such? First and foremost in the method employed in learning them. There are two main methods of learning languages, and these two methods correspond to the two fundamental activities of our intellect. I have already told you in the previous lecture that the science which treats of our intellectual digestion, so to say, and is alone capable of settling the educational value of any given course is Psychology; it is natural, therefore, that we should now summon that science to our aid. The two fundamental activities of which I speak are termed, in contemporary Psychology, *association* and *apperception*. Both processes alike aim at the reception and the reproduction of intellectual material by our mental organism; but one of these processes entails a greater degree of attention than the other. If a word, which I have chanced to hear under certain definite circumstances, on the repetition of these same circumstances rises spontaneously into my memory, then we ascribe this result to *association*. If, however, in both reception and reproduction, an effort of memory has to be made, then we name the corresponding activity of our mind *apperception*.

Now let us apply what has been said to the process of learning languages. It is by means of association, that is to say, by the merely passive process of attention, that a man masters, first of all, his own mother tongue. By this process, however, he gains nothing but a mere mechanical knack, so to say, which enables him, indeed, without effort to master and use all the treasures at his disposal in the etymology, vocabulary, and syntax of his own language; while, at the same time, he is unable to account for the reasons why he uses them just in that particular way. In other words, he is ignorant of the structure of the language. All modern languages are learnt by the process of association by those whose mother tongues they are; and it is just because this method of rapidly learning a language is so easy and practical that it should be applied, as far as possible, to foreign languages as well. Latterly the method of association for acquiring foreign languages has found its way into our schools also, and there seems no doubt that, however it be called, it will come in time to be the dominating method. First, however, of course, it must be purged of the extravagancies which still burden it.

The method of *apperception* is the opposite to that of *association.* By this method we, first and foremost, study the structure of a language; we master with full consciousness the peculiarities of its etymology, vocabulary, and syntax, and step by step we learn to understand and form first simple sentences, then progressively harder ones, and finally periods and series of periods. By this means we arrive at not the mere mechanical readiness of which I spoke, but at a scientific knowledge of the structure; for instance, a learner will master the rules of the sequence of tenses long before he begins to use the proper tense in a given case without hesitation or mistake. But if so, it follows that all that is said about the utility of the study of language applies only to the method of apperception.

How little intellectual influence is exercised by the method of association we may see at once in the case of waiters in foreign hotels; they talk quite glibly in several languages which they have learnt by this method. Now, we have seen that we all learn our mother tongues by the method of association, and by it alone. The method of apperception is, indeed, quite impossible in this case, for the language is learnt at an age when the mind is as yet too undeveloped to assimilate anything by apperception. We have seen, further, that modern foreign languages, in the acquisition of which the method of apperception is by itself quite possible, are ever tending more and more to the adoption of the method of association, and in process of time will employ it altogether. We have no call to check this movement, for the main object in learning modern languages is to be able to speak, or at least to read, them readily and easily, and this end is certainly attained more readily and easily by the method of association. Hence it will be understood that all that has been said about the educational utility of the study of languages applies solely to the study of the ancient languages.

Before proceeding further, let us review the results already gained. We have proved the educational value of ancient languages in general; we have not proved that these ancient languages must necessarily be Greek and Latin; and we have not proved that both must be regarded as essential and not merely one of the two. We need hardly trouble to notice any objection raised on the former of these grounds, although we unfortunately hear it often enough insisted on. In the first place, however, whoever wishes to introduce into our secondary schools the study of ancient Hebrew or of Sanskrit in place of Latin and Greek shows that he has no idea of the nature of either group of languages. In the second place, the weak point of all such substitutes for the classical languages consists in the fact that each one of them is proved to be suitable to a certain degree in some one feature only of these which collectively form the strength of the classical languages. Accordingly, if we put all such proposed substitutes together, so as to form an equivalent at all points for Latin and Greek, their sum will prove far more burdensome than the two classical languages alone, and the result will be, instead of a harmonious whole, a disordered chaos of disjointed and unconnected scraps of knowledge. The second objection that I indicated, namely, that we have not as yet proved the necessity of learning both languages, is correct; but correct only "as yet."

Now to proceed. It stands to reason that those languages must be the most intellectually fruitful and must best repay their acquisition by the apperceptive method, which firstly, by virtue of their organic structure, afford the greatest amount of intellectual nourishment; and which, secondly, by virtue of their psychological peculiarities, form the most desirable complement to the mother tongue. Let us deal with the second desideration first. I repeat once more, gentlemen, what I have already told you: Psychology answers in the sphere of things intellectual to Physiology; and Chemistry is replaced by what I called the *psychological science of Knowledges*. With the aid of these two sciences we shall be able some time or other to analyse fully what I have, with more truth than poetry, termed our intellectual digestion. I have given you already an example of the application of Psychology to our subject when I spoke to you of association and apperception. I must now give you an example to illustrate what I mean by the "Psychological science of knowledges" in its application to linguistics.

We differentiate in languages two kinds of elements. In the first place, such as express visibility and generally objects of immediate sensation; in the second place, those that express the results of our reflective powers. The first we call *sensuous*, the second *intellectual* elements; that distinction, as you will see, is in touch with the distinction between natural and abstract elements, but does not coincide altogether with it. Judging by the predominance of these or those elements in languages, we differentiate languages also into similar groups; that is to say, some languages we call sensuous, others intellectual. Now, if you were to construct a table from this point of view indicating progressively the languages akin to our own, in which the first language on the list should be that which appeals most to the intellect and least to the senses, and the last language that which appeals least to the intellect and most to the senses, we should find at the two extremities of our line of progression the Latin and the Russian languages respectively. The contrast between them is shown most strikingly in the system of their respective inflections.

The sensuous character of a language betrays itself most evidently in the so-called system of "aspects."* This scheme of "aspects" reproduces for us the immediate impression received by the organs of the senses. As contrasted with this, the intellectual character of a language finds its expression by its tenses on the one hand, and by its moods on the other. The tenses are the result of an assorting memory and of reflection.† The *memory* preserves the pictures of events in correct historical perspective, projecting these, as it does, not on one common background, but on several, in their due and natural sequence. *Reflection*, again, creates similar scenes for future events as well. Remember how you had to translate into Latin a sentence like the following: "If you will come to me, we will go for a walk." The Latin for "you will come" is *venies;* therefore a Russian [or an Englishman] is tempted to write *cum ad me venies ambulabimus*, which would be wrong. For the act of *coming* precedes the *walk*. Two different shades of the future are denoted; we have to employ the "Futurum exactum," or so-called perfect future, and say, "Cum ad me *veneris* ambulabimus." This differentiation the Russian language does not express, but blends all the steps of the sequence in the common background of the *Future*. Latin, on the other hand, expresses it,

* These "aspects" are strongly represented in the Russian verb, which differentiates in form lasting, completed, repeated and isolated action.

† Cf. Weise, "Characteristics of the Latin Language," Chap. I.

and demands of you that when you write in Latin you should summon reflection to your aid. Thus it is that in our northern lands of mist the different optic distances are commonly merged in one common grey background, thereby contrasting with the sharp outlines of southern climes with their sunny glow and their distinctness.*

In this respect the moods are even more instructive. They are the result of the same reflective faculty, which is not satisfied with the simple statement of the naked truth as it is conveyed to us by our senses, but which carefully differentiates the various relations in which the given action stands to the truth, beginning with their absolute correspondence, continuing with the idea of probability, then followed by that of mere possibility, and concluding with their absolute difference. Tenses and moods are particularly fully developed in the two classical languages—the tenses remarkably so in Latin, and the moods in Greek; the *aspects,* on the other hand, are, especially in Latin, but feebly developed. In Russian, however, the tenses are hardly marked at all, the moods are entirely wanting; but the aspects have arrived at a stage of development such as is found in no other language.

Thus the ancient languages are primarily intellectual, and as such they form a desirable complement to Russian, which is primarily sensuous. It is particularly interesting to observe in this connection that our opponents, when confronted

* This sentence is not in the second edition.

with the contrast to which we have alluded, enlist this very contrast in their service. "Latin," so they say, "in its construction stands in sharp opposition to Russian; consequently we Russians do not need it at all." The fallacy of this syllogism will at once appear if we transfer its application to more material ground. Just imagine an economist who would argue thus: "Russia is pre-eminently an agricultural country; it follows that it is unnecessary to import industrial products; nothing but wheat need be imported. Britain, on the other hand, is pre-eminently an industrial state; hence she requires the importation of industrial products; but she needs no wheat." In such a case, moreover, history comes to the support of theory and confirms its conclusions. In every modern language Latin has supplied the place of the instructor who has "intellectualised" it; and after this first schooling and intellectualisation they passed, as we have seen, with its help again through a second period also, that bestowed on them artistic finish. The creator of German prose style was Lessing; of French, most likely of all writers, Balzac the elder; of Italian, Boccaccio; all three chose deliberately Latin examples as their models and followed in particular Cicero.

Now let us proceed to the first point which I proposed to you. I maintain that the classical languages must be held to be the most fruitful and advantageous for the process of "apperceptive" learning, because, owing to their structure, they afford the greatest amount of intellectual nutriment.

To prove our point we must scrutinise somewhat more closely the "unfruitful waste" of the ancient languages, as our opponents are wont to call it. Let us begin at the beginning. In the very first lesson in Latin the scholar, to his great relief, finds that the reading presents no difficulties, owing to the nearly absolute correspondence of the pronunciation with the print, of the sounds with the letters. There is no modern language in which this correspondence is so complete; indeed, from this point of view alone Latin deserves to be the first foreign language introduced to a boy. Surely it is far more natural to pronounce at once the word *est* as it is written, and not till the study of French has been entered on to learn the later mutilated pronunciation, *eh*, than to teach from the outset that one and the same word is pronounced *eh*, but written, for some unintelligible reason, *est*.

Before proceeding further, however, let us ask ourselves how much advantage the lucidity of the Latin language has brought us as expressed in the correspondence of its pronunciation and orthography. Only that the pronunciation may be learned with no trouble? Not so. In one of my future lectures I mean to speak to you on the idea, so fashionable nowadays, of "lightening" school work, and to draw your attention to the serious dangers of a social character—yes, gentlemen, of a *social character*—which this process entails. All school work is of two kinds: *educative* work and *non-educative* work. By educative work

I understand work which constrains you to use your mind, as you bring a special instance under a general rule. Such work, too, has its value from a moral point of view, teaching you, as it does, to appreciate the force of law, and not of caprice, as your guide, and to accept nothing on credit without good grounds on which to base belief. Now, remember all the trouble which it cost you to learn the orthography of the French language, owing to its non-correspondence with the pronunciation. Can you call such work as this intellectually or morally educative ? Why is a word pronounced as *eh* written sometimes *et*, sometimes *est*, sometimes *ait ?* What is the reason of the appearance of the unpronounced and unnecessary letter *g* in *doigt*, a finger ? Why have the words *honneur*, *labeur* no final *e*, while we find it in *demeure* and *heure ?* To these questions no answer is given ; the only sufficient reason which can present itself to the student is " that my teacher said it was so," or " so it says in the text-book." Of course, there are satisfactory reasons for all these apparent discrepancies ; but these reasons must be sought in the Latin language. The orthography of the words *et*, *est*, and *ait* is perfectly intelligible to any one who is aware that they come from the Latin words *et*, *est*, *habeat*. The superfluous consonant *g* in *doigt* will puzzle no one who knows that *doigt* is derived from *digitus*.* Again, no one can be misled in the orthography of the words in *eur*(*e*) who knows that in Latin the stem of the

* In O. Fr., however, written *doit*.

words in the first category mentioned—as *honor, labor*—terminates in a consonant; that of those in the second category in a vowel—as *hora, mora.*

These are simple facts, and in all that I have said I have not had the least desire to depreciate the value of the French language. But we have in our mind's eye a pupil who is supposed to be learning French without knowing Latin. He is sensible of no general law which may guide him; he feels merely an arbitrary caprice; and I personally deplore every hour wasted in such learning. It neither develops nor frees the intellect; on the contrary, it crushes and stifles its innate desire to find law and a reasonable cause in every particular case. And precisely for this reason I count it one of the great merits of the Latin language, and of Greek as well, that from the outset they liberate the learner from this toil and drudgery.

The same lucidity of construction which facilitates our understanding of the principle of cause and effect—so important for the development of the mind—appears in later stages as well, beginning with the accidence. There are five declensions in Latin. Why precisely five? I ask a pupil to form the genitive plural in all these five consecutively: mens*a*rum, hort*o*rum, turr*i*um, stat*u*um, di*e*rum; and then the ablative singular: mens*a*, hort*o*, turr*i*, stat*u*, di*e*. The same vowels meet us, and each declension has its own. Now the boy sees why the Latin language has five declensions. It is because it has five vowels. But besides vowels there are also consonants. And so in Latin we have the genitives : re*g*um, capi*t*um, dolo*r*um. It is clear that these and similar words are declined like those in *i*, and that the two classes taken together form the so-called third declension. Now the pupil understands why certain words of the third declension have in particular cases the terminations *-i*, *-ium*, *-ia* ; whereas others have *-e*, *-um*, *-a*. Then follows a natural question: "How is it in this respect with Russian?" And the teacher will reply that, strictly speaking, it is the same as in Latin. In Russian, however, it is not so obvious, because the terminations have become abbreviated. "But when the time comes for you to learn Church Slavonic," the teacher will say, "you will find that in the Slavonic group of languages also the declensions depend on the final vowel of the stem, that they also possess stems ending in *-a*, *-o*, *-i*, and *-u* (only not in *-e*), and that in them also stems ending in a final consonant have become partially fused with stems in *-i*.

The same phenomenon appears in the system of the Latin conjugations : am*a*re, doc*e*re, stat*u*ere, fin*i*re. The consonants are attached to the *u* stems ; re*g*ere and scri*b*ere are conjugated like stat*u*ere. But why do we find no stems in *o*? Because they are unnecessary with the *a* stems ; the verb firm*a*re does common duty for firm*u*s and firm*a*. All this does not belong to a scientific and historical grammar of Latin. It is merely a common-sense grammar for a schoolboy. That very character it bears tends to convince him that law, and not caprice, reigns supreme in the Latin language, and that every phenomenon in that language has its intelligible cause. Try now to obtain the same results in German, with its senseless 'strong,' 'weak,' and 'mixed' declensions, or with the French conjugations and their equally senseless and arbitrary terminations in *-er*, *-ir*, *-oir*, and *-re!* To apprehend any method in French I must once again call Latin to my assistance, and refer the French verbs *aimer*, *finir*, *devoir*, and *vendre* to their Latin originals *amare, finire, debere,* and *vendere.* It is with good reason that Vinet, that great master of the French language and literature, says, "Le latin c'est la raison du français," implying thereby that French, taken by itself, has no *raison,* and as a language no nutriment to offer to the intellect. That is why there is every reason for learning French, and indeed all modern languages, by the associative method. The apperceptive method should be reserved for those whose structure makes it worth while.

"But the exceptions?" you will say. Yes, of course. If we only were able, we would make Latin without any exceptions whatever. As it is, we may fairly congratulate ourselves that they are so few. Just recall the easiest of the Russian declensions—namely, that of the feminines in *-a*. There you have words absolutely similar in form and accentuation which yet make three different differently declined types. Or, again, take another easy declension—the masculines with the hard final sign. Their monosyllables actually fall into four types. If, then, you proceed—and the apperceptive method compels you to do so—to take any one of these types as 'the rule,' you will soon see what infinite series of exceptions will present themselves. Then recall the genders of the French, and especially the German substantives, and you will readily agree that the exceptions to the rules in Latin are comparatively very few.

Still, these exceptions do exist, and as far as they exist they increase the difficulty of mastering languages by the apperceptive method. What has the classical school to say to these exceptions? As a school with a serious purpose, it demands intellectual work from its pupils, but only as far as this work is educative and profitable. Now it considers the learning of exceptions as necessary, indeed, in view of further study, but as unprofitable in regard to intellectual development. For this reason it has lightened, absolutely as far as is possible, the burden of learning them. The celebrated economist Bücher has given in his "Work and Rhythm" his theory of the value of Rhythm as a national economical asset owing to its power of easing the strain of work. He finds in the primitive meaningless and merely rhythmical melodies sung by workmen one of the main sources—he actually says the only source—of poetry. This book was not yet written at the date which I have in mind; still, the facts, which Bücher was the first to examine with such care, were recognised even before his time. Further, the classical school perceived that they had to do not with adults, but with children nine or ten years old, for whom the practice of committing to memory meaningless rhythmical concatenations of words is a physical necessity. We need only remember that this is just the age when children are so fond of playing at "counting," as they call it, when they keep on repeating some gibberish or other destitute of meaning, but of a rhythmical form. The classical school, then, utilised the psychological facts to which I have alluded—namely, first the power of rhythm to facilitate effort, especially in regard to memory, and, secondly, the readiness of children to learn by heart rhythmical series of words. So it found a way out of the difficulty into which the existence of exceptions had brought it. Its anxiety to facilitate the process of learning them caused it to draw up the celebrated rhyming rules with which our opponents are never tired of reproaching us. At a later period the aims of education underwent a change, so that it became possible to abbreviate these rules to a considerable extent. In this shortened form they have proved so far the best method for the assimilation of the necessary matter. I have employed them myself when I was master of a lowest class. I remember well how the comical rhymes and the droll juxtaposition of the curious words evoked rounds of healthy boyish laughter from my pupils, especially when at the close of the lesson I made them repeat the rhyming rules in chorus. I consider a spirit of hearty cheeriness to be a supremely healthy symptom—to use a doctor's expression—in the education of young schoolboys, and so the close of the lesson came always to be regarded as a kind of amusing game. Had our school doctor agreed to test the bluntness of my boys' nerves after these lessons, I think that he would have been quite satisfied!

I have now indicated the nature of Latin accidence. Let me add a few words about that of Greek. It may be regarded as the culminating point of linguistic structure, adding as it does the important department of Phonetics. Greek alone offers a properly developed phonetic system; it alone introduces us to such important linguistic phenomena as the contraction of vowels and the combination of consonants, by the appreciation of which the structure of language becomes still clearer and more intelligible. The Greek conjugational system is a triumph of such perspicuity. It is in Greek alone that this feature of language can be treated synthetically. Let me show a pupil not fully constructed forms, but merely their component elements. I tell him that the stem remains generally unchanged, but that different appendages are attached to this stem which express the time (the so-called tense characteristics), the mood (the so-called connecting vowels), the person and the number (the terminations). I teach him the way to use these different elements; I draw his attention to the fact that, when the action lies in the past, this is expressed by the prefixing the augment, and that its accomplishment is denoted by reduplication; and after this a pupil will rarely need my aid to form the whole system of the conjugation. And I need hardly say that this process of resolving linguistic forms into their elements explains to him not merely the Greek language—it illuminates for him similarly the structure of any given language, in fact, of language in general. From this point of view we may say that Latin accidence reveals to the learner the anatomy of language, and Greek its chemistry. The two combined give him a clear insight into its origin and construction. Language will not seem after this training a mass of purely conditional and arbitrary rules, but a natural phenomenon, governed by law and majestic in its adherence thereto. Every one can be readily persuaded of the importance of reaching such a view. Let us remember that language is part of the Nature which, indeed, environs us everywhere and always. Now, if we show a boy how this part also is governed by law, and train him to observation in this field, we encourage in him the true scientific spirit which fits a man for any scientific pursuit. I cannot dwell on this consideration any longer; but I would refer you to the "Introduction to Philosophy" of Fr. Paulsen. The author proves that even the theory of evolution, on which Natural Science plumes itself so proudly in our day, was applied originally by W. Humboldt to the Latin language, and only at a later period transferred to the phenomena of material nature. I may add that this book cannot be too warmly recommended to those who entertain the mistaken idea that the method of scientific research is inseparably bound up with its material. However, the incorrectness of this view is clear to all those who have ever studied the history of any science or who have themselves worked on scientific methods.

But enough for to-day. The branch of knowledge, whose importance I have tried to show you, occupies but a small place even in what we may call "school Antiquity," not to mention the system of "Antiquity" in general; that is to say, the system of those departments of knowledge which are connected with the ancient world. Still, it is the first ground which a man who approaches the domain of Antiquity has to cover, and this is the reason why we are met in discussing it by so many questions of principle which demand to be cleared up at any cost. On the other hand, this is the very branch of classical education which is most reviled. All our opponents reproach us more bitterly than for any other reason with the grammar of the ancient languages, "that barren desert," as they call it. I have tried to point out to you that this supposed desert brings forth its fruits, and, what is more, fruits which, if not always sweet to the taste, are always sound and healthy both intellectually and morally.

And with that I close to-day. In my next lectures I hope to proceed somewhat more quickly. We may do so without fear of loss to our subject, as I shall devote myself to aspects of Antiquity which are more attractive in form as well as in subject.

LECTURE III

BEFORE beginning my third lecture on the educational value of Antiquity, it may be useful to recall briefly to your memories the contents of the two first lectures which you heard a fortnight ago. We saw, first of all, that the unfriendly attitude of a large section of society toward Antiquity ought not to be considered as of decisive importance. That conscious unfavourable judgment, the product of delusion and deception, is of no account as compared with the unconscious favourable judgment of the same society, which has cherished classical education now for from fifteen to twenty centuries. The great " I " is more important than the small one. We have also seen that the educational value of Antiquity must be accepted as a fact on the ground of the data of our experience, quite independently of our success or failure in answering satisfactorily the question of wherein it consists. It is with classical education as with bread. The value of bread was accepted as a fact on the ground of the data of human experience long before the physiology of digestion and Organic Chemistry had demonstrated it by analysis. After passing briefly over certain other questions of principle we came to our main problem—namely, to explain as adequately as possible the educational value of classical study. We saw that three elements form the classical curriculum in our secondary schools—namely, the structure of the two languages, passages selected for reading from the best productions of ancient literature, and instruction of various sides of Antiquity through the medium of ancient history, and so forth. We turned our attention to the first of these elements, the structure of the two languages with its three divisions—accidence, vocabulary, and syntax. I endeavoured to show you that the educational value of the ancient languages as such consists for us mainly in the fact that they are acquired not by the method of association, but by that of apperception, which is suitable for application to the ancient but not to modern languages. I showed that their value lies, secondly, in the fact that their psychological peculiarities, as being intellectual languages, point to them as the most desirable complement to Russian, an essentially sensuous language. Thirdly, we saw that their structure provides the greatest amount of nutriment for the intellect. The value of this mental pabulum, so to say, afforded by the two classical languages we have established in the first instance for their accidence. We have seen that both Latin and Greek alike are almost entirely free from the indigestible ingredients which are produced by a dissimilarity between orthography and pronunciation and merely burden the memory.

We have seen, too, that Latin accidence, owing to its relative clearness, shows to the pupil the anatomy of language in general and teaches him thereby to regard language as a phenomenon of Nature subject to law. The so-called exceptions—those sources of perturbation for youthful minds—are relatively few; and the effort of their committal to memory can be lightened materially. I told you, also, that Greek accidence, owing to its still greater lucidity, permits us to analyse the language into its simplest elements, a process which I described as linguistic chemistry. Here we stopped. The characteristics belonging to the two other parts of the structure of the classical languages—namely, vocabulary and syntax—had perforce to be postponed to the present lecture.

But, gentlemen, before I set about this task I deem it fitting to communicate to you certain reflections aroused by the attitude of some of my audience to my first two lectures. My task was and is the appreciation of the educational value of a classical education. The appreciation, you will note, not the defence. I had no idea of standing forth of my own accord as their apologist. But such an apologetic element appeared and, indeed, must naturally appear of itself. When any feature of public life is attacked unfairly, a correct appreciation of it must involuntarily assume the appearance of an apology. This fact entails an awkward consequence. The calumniator is disposed to regard any protest raised against his calumnies as a calumny levelled against himself. To take an example: A student of Natural Science maintains that the study of Antiquity is valueless. I controvert him, and prove that, on the contrary, it is valuable in various ways. Well, says my opponent, so you hold that Natural Science is useless? Not at all, my scientific friend! That is far from being my opinion; quite the contrary. The difference between us lies just in this, that I understand and honour your science, while you apparently are incapable of honouring, that is to say understanding, mine.

I would repeat that the aim of these lectures is merely to point out the characteristics of my special branch of knowledge. Here and there I am forced by necessity to say a word in its defence and in my own; but throughout I am careful never to calumniate anybody or anything. I will express myself more clearly. I have not merely never had any idea of calumniating any one, I have never done so. I am fully justified in saying this, for I have pondered over every word of these lectures with that precaution kept firmly in view. If, however, any one deem himself aggrieved by anything that I have said, then I permit myself to observe to him that this feeling is the result of his own misinterpretation of my words, for which I am not to blame. I could not foresee such misinterpretations. Only one path, as I said, leads to truth; but the paths of delusion are in number as the stars in heaven. And now I must proceed with my subject.

The educational value of the accidence of the two classical languages we discussed in the preceding lecture—very cursorily, of course, for unfortunately lack of time prevents our going further than the merest rough outline. To-day it is the turn of Semasiology. This subject is confined in our secondary schools to the acquisition of Latin and Greek "words," and lasts during the whole course of instruction, accompanying, as it does, the perusal of each author. You may ask of what use it is. My answer is—of great and manifold use. I have in view, however, merely the generally educational value of the classical languages, and so I will not dwell on the importance of a knowledge of their vocabulary for the conscious appreciation of the Latin and Greek words which continue to live in modern languages, more especially in scientific terminology. Nor will I speak of the value of this knowledge as facilitating and making intelligible a study of the Romance languages, notably French. And yet it is just what I call its generally educational value which is most in dispute. What good is it, people ask, to be able to call a dog in Latin "canis," and in Greek *κύων*? Is my idea of a dog enriched thereby in the slightest degree? When I hear these assertions—and I often do hear them—I feel like the chemist who is told that water is one of the elements, or like the astronomer who has to listen to an account of the sun's revolution about the earth. I seem to breathe the air of a close, musty atmosphere, and I am convinced that all the most modern results of linguistic science have passed without leaving a trace, as far as my collocutor is concerned. W. Humboldt was perfectly right when he said that language is no mere machine for the understanding, but the very impress of the spirit and mental outlook of the speaker. Prince Vyazemski expressed the same thought in his verses: "Language is the confession of the people, revealing its nature, its soul, and its peculiar life." Let us take as an example the word which people commonly say on taking leave of each other: χαῖρε, "vale," "adieu," "farewell," "leb wohl." Here each language expresses a fresh idea, a fresh particle of the confession of the people who speak it. But, it may be asked, in what respect are the classical languages better than the modern in this connection? My answer is, that in the first place they are mastered by the apperceptive method, as has been previously explained, so that we feel consciously their peculiarities of vocabulary. The distinctive features of the modern vocabularies, on the other hand, which are learnt by the associative method, are not consciously apprehended. A Russian who speaks French will reflect as little on the word "adieu," which is ever on his lips, as on his own Russian word "proščáy." On the other hand, in Greek he is bound to learn that χαῖρε means properly "rejoice," and only secondly "good-bye." In Latin, again, he will be taught that "vale" is, strictly speaking, "be healthy" and then "good-bye." He will now catch some slight touch of the joyous spirit of

Greece and the sober, wholesome spirit of Rome. Then automatically, like a kind of ricochet, the question presents itself to him: And how is it in Russian? And he will begin to reflect on the meaning of our parting salutation, "prosti," "proščáy," that is to say, "pardon me"; and this scrap of the confession of his people will awake in him the consciousness that his mother tongue is indeed a noble one, instinct with soul and feeling. There you have one advantage of the knowledge of the classical languages, or rather two; for I consider that a constantly aroused desire to institute comparisons between my own language and those of the ancients is a second valuable element in classical Semasiology. This, however, is not all.

Its third merit is its lucidity. One of the Latin words of the third declension is *cor, cordis,* the heart. "Have we ever met with any word from the same stem?" I ask a pupil. "Yes—concordia." "What, then, is the proper meaning of concordia?" "The meeting of hearts." (A schoolboy will probably say: "When hearts are together," which is perhaps better still.) And thus an example shows the development of abstract from concrete conceptions. Following on this, like a ricochet, comes my question: "How does Russian express this?" And the boy, for the first time in his life, will begin to reflect on the word "soglásiyé." He will see in a moment that the word means, strictly speaking, "the union of voices"; and a further point will probably occur to him at the same time—namely, that Latin in this particular instance expresses perhaps more depth and feeling than the Russian. Try and obtain the same results with the French word "concorde." A boy will hardly recognise in it the word "cœur" at all. Or take the German "Eintracht." He will fail to understand this word, even though it be explained to him that "tracht" comes from "tragen."

The fourth point in which classical Semasiology is valuable for us may be inferred from Prince Vyazemski's words, which apply to the classical languages above all others, chiefly because they—and more especially Greek—developed of themselves without being influenced by other languages. I lay particular stress upon this point. Greek is quite an irreplaceable language for us, simply because it has developed independently. That does not mean, of course, that no foreign words whatever are to be found in Greek. Certainly there are some, mainly of Phœnician origin. They are, however, not only very few, but they have reference only to the foreign world and do not at all affect the spirit of the people. Nor do I speak here altogether of foreign words in the strict sense of the term. These bear an obvious mark of their foreign origin, and being more or less easily recognised, cannot mislead anybody. No, I mean such as have been translated from a foreign tongue into Greek, and so have found their way into the language by a purely external process, without having passed through the forge of popular consciousness. You will easily perceive that the greater the percentage of such words in a language, the less does that language reflect the consciousness of the people who speak it. Now, such words do not exist in Greek. Hence the entire Greek language, as it is, presents us with a reflection of the mind of the Greek people, so that, even had all Greek literature perished, we could restore a picture of this mind by the aid merely of a Greek dictionary. Modern languages, on the other hand, including Russian, offer no such possibilities. Indeed, Russian in particular contains such a number of these translated words that not merely the educated classes, but even the most ignorant peasants, cannot talk straight from the heart and conscience without them. For example, consider this very word "conscience."* Can the common people, can we, the educated classes, manage without it? Obviously not. But can we say that this word is the product of the national consciousness, or a fragment of the confession of the Russian people? No, gentlemen! This word did not grow up out of the consciousness of the Russian people. What makes up the word "sóviest"? Let us analyse it: "viest" comes from "viedaiyu," "I know." "Sóviest," then, from "so-viedaiyu," "I know with"? But we have no such word or phrase. We do not use the preposition "so,"

* Just as the word "gewissen" (= "mitwissen") was added by Notker Labeo to the German vocabulary, as a literal translation of the Latin word "conscientia," so the Russian word "sóviest" goes back to the word συνείδησις found in the New Testament.

"with," in this connection at all. We say, "I do not know sin behind myself," and not "I do not know sin with myself." How, then, has the word appeared in Russian? By a purely literary process, through a translation of the Greek word συνείδησις (Latin, "conscientia"), which occurs several times in the New Testament. But the word συνείδησις is a purely Greek word and conception. In Greek it is perfectly natural to say σύνοιδα ἐμαυτῷ κακόν τι ποιήσαντι, "I know in common with myself as with one who has done wrong." Do you understand what these words signify? This: When you did wrong, you took every precaution to hide it. You hid it from your fellow-men, and perhaps from the gods also. But do not comfort yourself with the idea that there are no witnesses. There is one who knows your deed "in common with" yourself, and that one is yourself, the divine principle of your soul. From this witness you can never escape as long as you live. For—I continue in Æschylus's words—"in the night, in place of sleep, mindful care knocks at the window of your heart, and even against your will you learn to be righteous." Man's mind is thus twofold: one portion, the earthly, defiles itself with sin; the other, the divine, becomes the stern witness and judge of the first. This second portion, which "knows in common with" ourselves, is our conscience. There you have again a particle of a people's confession. Yes, but it is a confession of the Greek people, forming one whole with the teachings of Æschylus and of

Plato, and not of the Russian people, who have adopted this word by a literal translation from the Greek. And we Russians possess plenty of such "translated" words; and they must be known if we would avoid ascribing to the soul of the Russian people that to which it has no claim. The conclusion to be drawn is clear. Paradoxical as it may seem, it is indispensable to know Greek in order to know Russian. Whoever clamours for the suppression of Greek and the strengthening of Russian at its expense proves by his very demand that he himself does not know the Russian language, its past, its soul.

However, the importance of Greek for the proper understanding of Russian is merely a side-issue. Our immediate theme is a different one—namely, the supreme importance of the classical languages as full and complete expressions of the souls of the peoples who spoke them. But Prince Vyazemski refers not merely to the soul. "Its soul and its peculiar life," says the last verse of those which I quoted. You may ask: "How does a nation's peculiar life fit in here?" Well, I shall explain this also by an example.

You all know the word *rivalis*, which has passed into the French as well. It means "a rival." But have you ever realised how the word came by this meaning? A boy in the lowest forms knows its derivation: *socialis* from *socius*, *rivalis* from *rivus*.*

* This derivation is called in question. See Walde, "Lateinisch - etymologischer Wörterbuch," s.v. The Romans, however, accepted it, though it may have been due to popular etymology.

Of course; but *rivus* means "a stream," so how did its derivative *rivalis* come to mean "rival"? It was in this way. In Italy, where heavy rain falls only rarely in the hot season, a system of artificial irrigation was employed in quite early times. The water of a stream or spring was drawn off by a canal, a *rivus*; ditches were connected with this canal and traversed the fields and meadows which had to be watered. The water was directed into these from the main canal by drawing up a hatch. When the earth had imbibed enough moisture the hatch was closed: "Claudite iam rivos, pueri, sat prata biberunt," says the herd in Vergil. Now you will easily understand that this water was prized highly in periods of drought. If a peasant on the slope above took too much water, his neighbour on the lower level would have too little. Hence arose frequent quarrels between the neighbours on the canals, the rivales. This is the original meaning of the word, and the Roman jurists employ it in this sense. Now, these disputes, this rivalry between the rivales, did not always remain confined to actions in civil law. There were also much more serious cases. Heavy rainfalls caused the canal, which received its waters from the hill springs, to rise in flood. Its waves burst forth tumultuously through the confining dams. Still a little, and it will reach the edge of our peasant's dam, or burst through it, deluge his fields, sweep away his cottage and ruin him . . . unless only it should break ere that into the fields of his neighbour on the other side of the canal and bring destruction to him. "Tua mors, mea vita." And so then he slinks off in the night; armed with his spade he creeps up to his neighbour's dam to break it through and let loose the fatal flood on the other's meadows gardens and buildings. But his neighbour is no more asleep than he. Scarcely have the first strokes of the spade sounded when the whole household assembles. Clubs, stones, and knives are caught up. A sanguinary conflict ensues—and between whom? Between the rivales. Now do you catch the process of change in meaning? Thus the "peculiar life" of the people reflects itself in the treasure-house of the language which it has created.

Now let us turn once again to the spirit of the people. This question is so interesting and important that I should like to illustrate it by a few other examples. What is the meaning of *potens?* "Powerful." And of *impotens?* Rarely "weak"; more commonly "passionate" or "uncontrolled." Now, in this you have the confession of a people who saw strength in reason and identified unreasonable passion with weakness. Again, πράσσω, "I do"; εὖ πράσσω, "I do well," and then, "I am happy." Here we have the germ of the Greek popular consciousness from which, later on, in direct continuation the moral philosophy of Socrates sprung, with its principle that virtue—that is to say, right conduct—is the necessary condition for happiness; and, still later, the Stoic ethics, which taught that virtue by itself makes a man happy. Consider next γιγνώσκω, "I recognise" or "understand." Now, συγγιγνώσκω means, properly speaking, "I understand together with," then "I pardon." What do you make of that? It implies nothing else than "tout comprendre, c'est tout pardonner." This humane principle, which sheds a lustre over the name of Madame de Staël, was recognised long before her time by the consciousness of the Greek people. But when a Christian prays to his God for forgiveness of sin, he cannot say to Him: "Understand them together with me." So in the Lord's prayer we find not the word **σύγγνωθι**, but ἄφες—*dimitte nobis peccata nostra*, "Send away from us our sins." The word "dimitte," it is true, has been ousted by the Italian "perdona," which remains down to the present day, but has the same signification: "give me beyond my deserts." I have given this last instance in view of the fifth reason for which we must value classical semasiology. This is because, thanks to it, we can enjoy a series of historical perspectives in miniature. These are both intrinsically interesting and valuable, and also encourage the historical spirit in the scholar's mind, that special mark of modern science which has bestowed the name "sæculum historicum" on the past nineteenth century.

If we now reckon up all the advantages which we have indicated, we must confess that they far outweigh the time taken up by the study of classical semasiology. I at least know from my own experience that this method can produce the deepest impression on pupils, calling into play, as it does, not merely thought, but feeling as well.

We have now fared happily through two divisions of the "barren steppe of the ancient languages." One has yet to come—the syntax. Many consider this the most terrible division of the three. The expression "intellectual gymnastics" is levelled against it especially. Our opponents apply this term to a feature selected as a favourite target of the jeers that they make do duty for arguments. Pray allow me to set against their opinion the judgment of a man who as a thinker possessed a knowledge of the process of thought, and as the father of modern psychology must be held an authority in the psychological questions which for the moment interest us—namely, Schopenhauer. In his treatise on languages and words* he says: "In translating into Latin we must denude the thought of the words which express it in the modern language. It must appear naked in our consciousness, like spirit without body; and then we must give it a completely new body of Latin words. These reproduce the original in a completely different form. What was, for example, expressed by substantives is now expressed by verbs, and so on. It is the employment of such a process of metempsychosis which develops real thought. It presents the same features as the *status nascens* in Chemistry. While a simple substance (*Stoff*) is leaving one

* "Über Sprache und Worte," § 299.

combination to connect itself with another, it manifests during this transition a special and peculiar force and activity. Similarly with the naked thought in its transition from one language into another. That consequently is the reason why the classical languages develop directly and strengthen the intellect." And this is the reason, I may add, why Fouillée could say with good reason: "Chaque leçon de Latin est une leçon de logique." In this he had in view a lesson of Latin syntax especially, but he might have confidently referred to Greek as well.

We shall have to return to Schopenhauer's views. For the moment let us notice that they touch merely one aspect of the subject. The second aspect, no less important than the first, lies in the fact that a lesson of Latin or Greek syntax is a lesson in Russian as well. Let me take an example. In running through the Greek syntax I give my scholars the following two sentences to translate: firstly, "He frequently prayed that he might be considered pious"; and secondly, "I pray God that He may soften the heart of my angry mother." The constructions are quite identical—two final sentences, a prayer "that . . . ." But in Greek they will be translated differently. In the first case we must use the conjunction *ἵνα* with the optative; in the second the infinitive without any conjunction. Why this difference? Because logic demands it. In the former sentence the expression "that he might be considered pious" is merely the object of the prayer and nothing else. In the latter, however, it is not merely the object, but the tenor also. Nekrassoff's peasant actually used the words: "God soften the heart of my angry mother"; whereas the tenor of the hypocrite's prayer is unknown, and indeed unimportant. Now, what do you think? Have I in this instance taught my pupils nothing but Greek syntax, or have I forced them to consider consciously the syntactical phenomena in Russian as well? But, it may be retorted, the same goal is attainable without Greek syntax. Go systematically with your pupils through Russian syntax; illustrate by apt examples the different logical categories embodied in corresponding grammatical categories—and the thing is done! My answer is—no; in this way the thing is not done! The pupil does not need to master any such fine points in Russian syntax to be able to understand Nekrassoff, who can hardly have known them himself. Yet he must know them to be able to translate properly into Greek or Latin phrases similar to the two cited above. But notoriously the most effectual educational artifice is the following: if any object which you have proposed as an end to your pupils fails to interest them by itself, you will only attain to it by making it a means to another end.

Generally speaking, syntax, as well as the other parts of grammar, should be studied just in the classical languages and not in Russian—and for the following reasons.

The first reason is that it is precisely in the ancient languages, and not in Russian, that syntax grew up and developed. It sits on Russian, accordingly, like a stolen cloak. How convenient are the grammatical categories in the Latin phrase *mihi pecunia deest,* and how unadaptable in the corresponding Russian expression, "with me not of money!" How will you explain to a boy where the subject is here, and where the predicate? The Roman said *grando laedit segetem;* the Russian says, "with hail lays waste the crops"—what is the subject? The Roman wishes to sleep, to the Russian it is wished to sleep. Everywhere one sees the difference between the intellectual character of the classical languages and the sensuous nature of Russian. And indeed everybody, I suppose, knows what a fruitless occupation are those grammatical analyses of Russian sentences, just because of the constant deviations of the living speech from grammatical forms.

Yes, gentlemen, Russian is, comparatively speaking, quite ungrammatical. Had it not been for the ancient languages from which the Russian grammar was borrowed, it would probably have simply remained without grammar. Perhaps many of you would not consider that a great loss; grammar is not a special favourite with schoolboys. But it is not sympathies or antipathies that we must consider. No one can deny that grammar is the first essay of logic applied to the phenomena of language, and that this fact constitutes the importance of grammar for educational purposes.

Now in syntax Russian is far less logical than the ancient languages for the same reason that makes it etymologically far less intellectual. It can be appreciated more readily from the psychological than from the logical point of view. Who knows but that if Russian had been left to itself we should have a psychological instead of the logical grammar that is in use at present, and employ in analyses of syntax not the terms "subject," "predicate," "principal sentence," etc., but expressions like "leading idea," "secondary idea," "closed structure," "open structure," "associative element," and so on! Of course, it is difficult to draw a detailed picture; the psychology of syntax is still in its veriest infancy. It promises to be an interesting science, but for educational purposes it cannot compare with the logical syntax which has been already duly tried. This latter is not a very tasty nourishment, but it is very healthy, and schools have full reason for prizing it and accordingly the ancient languages as well, from which, as I have said, it is most naturally derived.

Thus the superiority which the classical languages possess in regard to grammar forms the first reason why grammar itself, and syntax in particular, should be studied just in them.

The second and perhaps the principal reason is the entire purposelessness of grammar in the associative method of learning languages. The pupil is, of course, perfectly well aware that his making an etymological or syntactical analysis of a given extract does not cause him to understand it an iota better than he understood it before. Consequently these exercises leave no traces whatsoever on his intellectual development. On the other hand, in translating from Latin or Greek into Russian, one must ask oneself at almost every phrase: Where is the subject? Where is the predicate? What does *ut* express here—consequence or purpose? And so on. Here grammatical analysis does really seem a means to the understanding of the text, and not an end in itself. Here, accordingly, it is both intelligible and profitable.

And now, before I finish with syntax and grammar generally, I must observe that in my opinion our grammatical handbooks in both Greek and Latin need reform. This is not the place to speak about that reform; so I confine myself to the remark that the reformer's aim should be not so much their abbreviation, the throwing overboard their so-called ballast, as their adaptation to the educational end of the mastery of the ancient languages. The grammarian should give prominence to and develop that part of his material which is valuable for logical and psychological reasons. As far as possible, he should lighten the process of learning matter which has no value in itself and yet is necessary for the understanding of the classical texts. He should eliminate whatever is unnecessary in both these respects.

I now continue.

Next to the syntax of a language comes the

style. The study of style does not form an educational course by itself, yet it claims consideration indirectly through its connection with translations made from and into the classical languages. Style thus holds a middle position between grammar, on the one hand, and the study of literature on the other. What are we to say about it? The opinion of Schopenhauer which I quoted is just as applicable to style as to syntax, if not more so. If I translate the sentence, "Hannibalem conspecta mœnia ab oppugnanda Neapoli deterruerunt" by "the sight of the walls frightened Hannibal from attempting the siege of Naples," I may call this a literary translation as contrasted with the literal and impossible one, "the seen walls frightened Hannibal from the having-to-be besieged Naples." With the former rendering I gain, firstly, the conviction that over and above the mere substantives and verbs stand conceptions which in themselves are neither the one nor the other, though they are necessarily expressed, owing to the stylistic peculiarities of the language which we happen to be using, sometimes by the one and sometimes by the other. That is to say, I learn to distinguish the conceptions from the words in which they are expressed. Now, this lesson is an indispensable preliminary for philosophical thought, since, as Friedrich Nietzsche aptly remarked, "Every single word is a preconceived judgment."

In the second place such instances teach me to mark those stylistic peculiarities themselves to which I have just alluded. I discover by experience what is peculiar to Russian and what is not. Similarly with Latin. And of the unique character of Latin in this respect any one may convince himself by taking the trouble to translate the sentence which I quoted into any modern language. "L'aspect des murs," "der Anblick der Mauern." Everywhere substantives, just as in Russian. Latin, with its verbs, is unique; even Greek says τῆς πολιορκίας instead of "oppugnanda." And pray do not think that this remarkable preference assigned in Latin to verbs is a peculiarity of the grammar alone. No, it corresponds with the very process of thought in the Roman mind, which was of a practical and not of a theoretical or "substantial" character, and found its fullest expression in the Roman religion. As far as Roman religion was genuinely Roman, it was founded on the deification of actions, and in this sense it may be called an "actual" or practical rather than a "substantial" or theoretical religion. Who would have imagined that between two such different things as grammar and religion there could be so intimate a connection? And yet this is so, and the very fact proves once again the correctness of the phrase, which I have quoted so often, "Language is the confession of the people."

That is the first point. If, however, in this respect Latin, and I may add Greek also, affords a means for theoretical mastery of language and of languages in general, in another respect it may fairly be called a training school for the practical improvement of literary style. I must emphasise the fact that we are here on the firm ground of historical experience. As I have remarked already, it was precisely the Latin language on which the peoples of the West built and developed their literary prose by dint of hard study and conscious imitation. Even Russian literary prose style, as far as we may be said to possess it, is the result of the vigorous training undergone by our language in the pseudo-classical period. We possess it, however, only to a very limited degree. It may truly be maintained that the Russian language is still far from being fully developed, and has not yet found an artistic form to correspond to its native strength and flexibility. But you may ask what were the special peculiarities in virtue of which Latin was, and still may be, a teacher of style for us. I shall try in this instance also to give you as clear and short a reply as is possible; and so I choose from the many characteristics of Latin style one which is specially prominent—namely, the period.

In considering the period, I beg you first of all to rid your minds of one prejudice. If you think that it serves merely as the expression of a luxuriant style, or that it is a mere solemn peal, with more sound than sense, you are completely mistaken. No, the period offers to the thinker the necessary spacious unity for his thoughts. This is due to the complex mutual gravitation of the parts and, if I may use the expression, of the atoms of reflection which interest the writer's mind in any given case. The period is, indeed, a living organism, with an extremely definite subordination of its more important by-sentences to the principal sentence, and of the by-clauses of secondary to those of primary importance. Without this large unity the building up of an argument would be as difficult as complicated algebraic calculations would be but for the brackets. To gain this end the period must be perfectly lucid, and this lucidity is obtained through manifold variations in all its subordinate parts. There are three grades of subordination: main sentences, full by-sentences, and abbreviated by-sentences. The two first are common to the languages of all civilised peoples. But the perfection of language in regard to the formation of periods depends upon the presence and prevalence of the third grade—namely, the abbreviated by-sentences. In this respect German is the least perfect language of all those akin to our own. German, in fact, is a two-grade language, and scarcely permits the abbreviated by-sentence. The Russian sentence, "a man having never learnt," cannot be reproduced in German by an abbreviated by-sentence: "ein Mensch nie gelernt habender." A full relative clause is necessary: "ein Mensch, der nie gelernt hat." The Romance languages stand on a somewhat higher level; they permit the abbreviation of certain sentences, expressive of attendant circumstances, chiefly by means of "gerundial" constructions, "ayant appris," and so on. This permission, however, is not extended to relative and noun clauses. The Russian language stands higher still. It sanctions abbreviations of certain sentences denoting attendant circumstances by means of "gerundial" constructions, and of nearly all relative sentences by participial constructions. The abbreviation of noun clauses, however, is no more permissible in Russian than in the Romance languages. The highest grade is attained by the two classical languages; they abbreviate not only the sentences denoting attendant circumstances—Greek abbreviates all, Latin only some—but also the relative sentences, and this not merely in cases where the subject is the same as in the principal sentence, but even where the subjects are different. This is effected by the aid of the so-called ablative or genitive absolute. The noun clauses also are abbreviated by means of the accusative and infinitive construction. Thus, then, the classical languages, disposing as they do of all three grades, are the most perfect in the period formation, and of modern languages Russian approaches them most nearly.

But the advantages with which Nature itself has endowed the Russian language remain for the most part unexploited. The classical languages unfortunately have played no directly educative part in modern times in regard to Russian. In early Russian history, indeed, Greek was, as we have seen, the preceptor of Russian, for which we owe it thanks. It was just during the period of its influence that the strong points of style native to the Russian language were forged. But I am speaking of the development of our prose style in modern times, right up to our own day. Only think how large a percentage of our literature, using the word in the wide sense, is made up of translations from other languages. Can you believe that these works exercise no influence on our own tongue? Moreover, these translations are exclusively from French, German, and English; that is to say, from languages which, as being two-grade, stand on a lower level as to style than Russian. In other respects they may stand on a higher level; but that is not the point here. The translators, followed by the reading public, grow accustomed to forego the use of all the stylistic excellencies of their mother tongue. Thus they lower it to the level of the language from which they are translating, and the result is the impoverishment of the Russian language. There is another destructive force at work in the same direction as these translations—namely, the unhealthy endeavour to approximate the language of literature to the naturally slipshod language of conversation. And, indeed, since literary Russian has passed from the hands of authors into those of journalists, the danger of its impoverishment has sensibly increased.

I beg you, gentlemen, to reflect seriously on the considerations which I now adduce; what I say will doubtless be new to many of you. I implore you not to take upon their bare word the comforting assurances of my opponents who choose to term naturalness what I brand as impoverishment, and to prate about the charm of simplicity. In regard to naturalness, we have long ago got rid of the delusion derived from Rousseau—so fruitful in its time—which confounded naturalness with primitiveness. We have reverted to Aristotle's definition, that naturalness is to be sought not in immaturity, but in maturity. It is the full period that is natural to Russian, which by its nature is a three-grade language, and not the poverty of style common to West European languages and to conversation. And as for the charm of simplicity, if that captivates you, then, pray, give up chromatics in music and go back to the seven-stringed or even four-stringed lyre; give up harmonies and declare the air of "The three blind mice" strummed out with one finger to be the acme of all music! Renounce likewise the elaborate palette of Raphael or Rubens, or, to take our own countrymen, Répin or Vasnietsoff; return—as certain decadents are actually doing—to painting with four colours without any shading! All that offers the charm of simplicity. . . .

No, gentlemen! In your hands and in those of your contemporaries lies the future of your native language. Do you remember that in ancient Athens it was deemed the solemn duty of every citizen to bequeath to his son the fortune which he himself had received from his father undiminished or, if possible, augmented? Whoever neglected this duty was said, in the picturesque language of that time, to have "eaten up his patrimony," τὰ πάτρια κατεδήδοκεν, and was declared to have forfeited his rights. Reflect upon the stern verdict pronounced by modern France in the person of Taine against the French Academy of the seventeenth century for yielding to the cry for simplification and permitting the impoverishment of the rich vocabulary of Rabelais. And do you take heed that your posterity shall never say of you, in regard to the Russian language, that you have devoured your patrimony!

Of course, I do not mean you to conclude that I ask you to speak and write in "three-graded" periods everywhere and always. If I advise you to develop your physical strength, that does not imply, surely, that you should use both hands and strain all your might in order to hand your neighbour a cup of coffee. No, my plea comes to this, that the educated Russian ought to understand how to construct periods which are at once complex and clear; that is, in cases where the sense demands a period, where it appears essential for the full logical and psychological expression of his opinion or narrative. And it is precisely in this respect that classical study, if directed by teachers who know their business, is able to render substantial services to the Russian language. German and French prose are quite useless to us owing to their imperfections in the respects which I have indicated. Classical prose alone constrains us in the process of translation to employ all the strong points of style which Russian possesses. It alone can serve as a training school for our stylists, and so preserve the Russian language from the serious and irreparable losses which threaten its existence.

At this point, however, I foresee an objection of the following nature. How can one expect to derive any advantage from classical prose for Russian, when these wonderful champions of the classics themselves spoil it with their gems of style? Was it not they who created such expressions as "He inducted war" or "He was cut off in respect to his head"?

This objection is distinctly out of date. Of course, in days when classical instruction was entrusted to persons who knew Russian but imperfectly, you could expect nothing else. But if you leave such monstrosities out of account, what does the argument come to? Classical teachers do certainly avail themselves occasionally, for educational purposes, of a literal translation, which I may call a working-translation, on the analogy of the term working-hypothesis. Thus, for example, I could not explain to a pupil who is learning Latin, but has not yet mastered it, the difference in point of style between "Hannibalem conspecta mœnia ab oppugnanda Neapoli deterruerunt" and "the sight of the walls discouraged Hannibal from an attempt to besiege Naples" in any other way than by putting in parallel columns this literary translation and the working-translation—namely, "the seen walls discouraged Hannibal from the having-to-be-besieged Naples." Sometimes the teacher asks the pupil for a working-translation in order to be satisfied that the boy has worked independently, but that is a police precaution rather than an educative measure. But in all such sentences the working-translation is nothing more than a transitional step corresponding to a similar transitional step in the process of thought. It may happen, indeed, that a pupil gets no further than this stage; but that is the result of laziness or carelessness, which ought not to be tolerated. Our working-translation serves the same purpose as the negative in photography. It is just as necessary a transitional step, and just as little suitable to be counted a final aim or final result of our work.

But, I may be told, call them negatives or what you will, still these ugly working-translations exist, the scholar hears them, they are echoed unconsciously in his style, and so distort and mutilate it. No, I answer, they are not echoed in his style; if you think otherwise, show me a single example where Russian has been marred through the influence of the classics. You will not find one. The character of the classical languages is such that a pupil-language receives from them only healthy elements tending to intellectual and artistic improvement, and unconsciously discards all that would force it to forsake that mounting path. Can we say the same of modern languages? Ask the zealots for the purity of Russian how far they are pleased with the intermingling of French with Russian, a sensible result of which is seen in the celebrated Nijni-Novgorod French jargon. I am not speaking here of such disgraceful exhibitions of linguistic stupidity as the idiotic proverb, "He is not in his own plate," which Pushkin stigmatised long ago and which is still in circulation, a proverb which shows that its perpetrator knew no other meaning of the French "assiette" than the gastronomical one. No; let us forbear to dwell on that point. But what are we to say of phrases like "that event had place at such and such a time," "that settles me," "a bloody bath," "a state shock," and so on? Are they due to the classics? No. One may rather say that classical education, by virtue of that highly developed feeling for language which it imparts to its pupils, teaches us to mark their unnatural character and avoid them.

However, enough of style and of languages generally! Have I told you everything and developed all the points touched on? Far from it. I have not spoken of the important fact that only the classical languages enable us to trace, so to say, the history of the incorporation of thought in words. As we pass from Homer to Herodotus, and thence to Thucydides, Xenophon, and Plato, and from these to Demosthenes and finally to Cicero, we see how the spirit of language struggles with the material, how by means of successive integrations of the separate parts of language the spirit introduces order and graduated subordination into it, how it creates from the isolated independent sentence of the so-called "threaded" style (λέξις εἰρομένη), the unified centralised period, much in the same way as a unified centralised state is built up from various independent autonomous communities. All this and much besides I was forced to omit. Even as it is, I fear that I may have worn out your attention by this lengthy discourse on language. But, gentlemen, the disquisition was not disproportionately long, for you yourselves, as pupils of a secondary school, have spent much time in the acquisition of the two classical languages. You may be disposed to think that you have spent too much time. Well, I have undertaken to prove to you that, contrary to the opinion of many, the time which you have spent in the study of the classics has not been uselessly wasted. With this end in view I could not pass lightly over the advantages which you have gained from a study of the structure of the ancient languages as such.

But, of course, you were not made to learn Latin and Greek with a view to these advantages alone. Their chief value is that they open a direct entrance to ancient literature, and so lead us indirectly to ancient culture in its widest sense. My next object, therefore, is to elucidate the educational value of ancient literature, and I have devoted the following lecture—my second lecture to-day—to this purpose.

LECTURE IV

IN passing from the subject of the classical languages to that of ancient literature I feel the pleasant sensations of a man who, but lately proscribed by public opinion, finds himself invested with, if not all, at any rate some of a citizen's rights. A considerable part of the modern world, even in Russia, recognises the importance of the study of classical, and especially of Greek, literature, only it imagines that the original texts are not in the least degree necessary for this purpose, that we may be content with translations.

When I had the honour to be a member of the Commission on Secondary Schools, the question of improvements in the programme of our "Modern" schools was raised, and the enlightened supporters of this most necessary and, indeed, indispensable type of schools expressed their desire that the study of classical literature—of course, merely in the form of translations—should be added to the curriculum. Should this idea be realised, the difference between the classical and the modern school in regard to our present question would consist mainly in this, that the former would acquaint its pupils with the same works in the original as the boys in the latter would peruse in translations. Now, must we admit the superiority of the classical school in this point of difference, and if so, why? In other words, can translations take the place of originals, and if not, what constitutes their inferiority? This is a question that I cannot pass over in silence; but do not be afraid that it will divert us from our subject. No, I am convinced, and I hope to convince you of the truth of my opinion, that the treasures of ancient literature may be divided into those which do not suffer by translation and those which are inseparably bound up with the form of the original. Thus the answer to the question just proposed gives at the same time one of the characteristics of classical literature.

As you will have seen from what I have said, I am no implacable enemy to translations. I have myself appeared in the rôle of a translator; I have published a large volume which I venture to hope may occupy not the lowest place among modern works of this nature. And it is precisely for this reason that I know what a translation can, and what it cannot reproduce. Whoever advises you to be satisfied with a translation instead of the original shows no more judgment than if he were to say: "Why trouble to go to the Conservatorium to hear Beethoven's or Tschaikovski's symphonies when you can hear them much more comfortably at home from a piece set for the piano?" You know that this is so, and yet not so. The piano setting certainly gives you something, but not everything; and the more artistic and profound any masterpiece of symphony is, the less can it be replaced by a piano setting. The delicacy of motive and of form are gained by a bold use of the peculiar qualities of each single instrument, and these cannot be reproduced by the piano. That is the case with translations also. Take the first words of Cæsar: "Gallia est omnis divisa in partes tres," "All Gaul is divided into three parts." The translator reproduces the original fully; nothing in the Latin is omitted. Take, on the other hand, the cry of Thetis in Homer when she hears of the sad fate that has overtaken her son Achilles: *ὢ μοι δυσαριστοτόκεια*, "Woe to me, who have to my sorrow borne the noblest hero in the world." In this instance also I reproduce all the sense; but in order to give the full meaning of the single word in the original I have had to use no less than twelve,* and you will easily perceive how this watering-down process weakens the force of the original. Take, finally, Pericles' characterisation of the Athenians in his funeral speech in Thucydides: *φιλοκαλοῦμεν μετ, εὐτελείας, καὶ φιλοσοφοῦμεν ἄνευ μαλακίας.* The translator throws up his hands in despair. He understands, of course, that the words are applied to a highly artistic nation fully capable of marking the contrast between artistic beauty of form and excessive richness of material, a nation of thinkers strong enough to withstand the solvent action of thought on the will. All that he under-

* The Russian needs only eight; in general, Russian is distinctly crisper than English.

stands, but the task of reproducing these two criticisms in the form of an antithesis so terse, so sonorous, so apt as that of Thucydides, presents itself to the conscientious translator as an utter impossibility.

Thus we must neither despise translations nor count them adequate substitutes for the originals. Schopenhauer, speaking of classical literature, maintains that they bear the same relation to the originals as chicory to coffee; some one else says that they give us only the wrong side of the carpet. This is, perhaps, too strong. It would be more correct to say that the character of the ancient languages is so peculiar that any translation from a classical author into a modern language would bear much the same relation to the original as a wooden model of the human body in an anatomical museum bears to the real body. Translations and models alike give us a general idea of the structure and contents of the original, but the more delicate details are lacking. Even these models, however, are of various degrees of merit. Some are really artistic and undeniably useful; others, again, are of coarse uncouth make and give quite a distorted idea of the original. The vast majority of Russian translations are unfortunately of this class; there are very few which give even a hint of the artistic. Well, and what? We must only wish that it were otherwise and do our best to improve matters; more we cannot do. Still, however perfect a translation may be, the rule, none the less, holds good that the classics can be interpreted and mastered in all their branches only in the original texts, just as the structure of the tissue of our bodies can be studied after nature alone and not by the aid of wooden models.

And yet this very method of interpretation has its usefulness called in question by some. Is it not really better, they ask, to read ten books of Livy in a translation than one in the original? You will understand that I am speaking now of the so-called exegetical method of reading the classics which is in vogue in our secondary schools. Does this method present any advantage, and if so, what?

At this point I must, first of all, bring before you the question of the moral aspect of education. I hesitated long as to whether I should speak to you about this point. Persons whose opinion I value highly warned me to refrain, and I must admit myself that it would have been more prudent to follow their advice. But prudence is not always compatible with a service to truth, and so I resolved, cost what it might, to confide to you my own views on this matter, for I attach a very great importance to them. I hope that you will understand and appreciate them better than some of my former audiences. At any rate, I beg you to pay particular attention to what I propose to say to you.

What is, first of all, meant by the moral element in education?

Neither science nor a course of teaching pursues moral aims directly. Their object is the attainment of truth, but a knowledge of the truth by itself does not make a man more moral. No, not the knowledge of the truth, but the path whereby that knowledge is attained, the effort we make over ourselves to accept it—there is where you must find the moral element of science and teaching. You may allow that the earth goes round the sun—there is nothing moral in that; if, however, you were of a different opinion to begin with, and then later on bowed before the truth after becoming acquainted with your opponents' proofs, then that was a moral achievement. The collision of the truth with the human mind stimulated one moral quality in the latter—namely, truthfulness. "I began by disputing with you, but now I see that I was wrong." Such is the motto of truthfulness in this case, and a course of teaching which produces such results I venture to call moral. This, then, constitutes the moral aspect of education. Bearing it in mind, let us now review the courses of instruction in our secondary schools. I would like you to notice that the relation of any given course to morality may bear one of three characteristics: favourable, unfavourable, or indifferent. A course of instruction which improves and strengthens the character is called "moral"; one which affects character unfavourably, "immoral"; one which affects it in no way at all, "non-moral." As I have explained in what sense I understand the word "morality" here, I trust that it will occasion no misunderstandings. I request my opponents, if there be any such in this room, to note my explanation carefully and refrain from any equivoques about my word "morality," however strongly they may be tempted to indulge in them.

And so, what is the relation between educational subjects and morality?

Let us begin with ancient literature studied directly in the originals; in fact, with what is commonly called the reading of the classics. I put myself in the teacher's place; I have before me the text which it is my duty to expound, and, mark, each pupil also has his text before him. I shall explain what this implies. By giving each pupil the text, I supply him at the same time with a common field for our observations and investigations. On this field I shall be guide, but nothing more. I grant him both the right and opportunities of checking me; and we are both controlled by a higher power—namely, the truth. I shall choose an example from Horace: "Scribendi recte sapere est et principium et fons."

A dispute arises between a pupil and myself as to the word to which *recte* is related. He refers it to *scribendi*, and translates: "To be wise: that is the first principle and the source of good writing." It has struck me somehow that *recte* goes closely with *sapere*, so that the translation will run: "To think correctly: that is the first principle and the source of writing." The pupil refuses to be convinced. "The cæsura," he objects, "lies between *recte* and *sapere* and divides them, so that on this ground alone it is more natural to connect *recte* with *scribendi*. The sense of the passage also demands this interpretation, for intelligence is the source not of all writing, but only of what is good and correct." "That is true," I reply; "but the cæsura often divides words which are connected in sense"—here I cite instances—"so that this consideration is of secondary importance. As for your other plea, incorrect writing, as such, does not occur to the poet to discuss." "Still," rejoins my pupil, "it seems to me that my interpretation has more to say for itself than yours." "No," I answer, "for according to your version *sapere* has no attribute, which it obviously needs. It is in itself an indifferent word, signifying originally 'to have a certain taste,' compare *sapor* and French *saveur*, and afterwards coming to mean 'to have certain intellectual faculties.' So to gain the meaning of 'to be wise' it needs an attribute—namely, the word *recte*, which you would separate from it." "How, then, does it come about," asks my pupil, "that the participle *sapiens*, a derivative from *sapere*, has the positive meaning of 'clever' and not the indifferent signification of 'a person of certain intellectual faculties'?" "That is no proof," I answer, "for the participles of indifferent verbs, which have passed into the category of adjectives, often assume a positive meaning; thus from the indifferent word *pati*, 'to bear' or 'suffer,' we get *patiens*, 'the person who can bear well, who is patient, long-suffering.' And kindly give me an example where the verb *sapere* alone without an attribute has the positive meaning, 'to be wise.'" For the moment my pupil is silenced, but next lesson he brings forward, as an example in his favour, another quotation from Horace: "Sapere aude," "Dare to be wise." "Yes, that is the case," I confess, "I was wrong." I adduce this instance inasmuch as it was an incident of my own, now long past, experience as a young teacher, and also because Oscar Jäger, the well-known German authority on education, recalls something similar in his recollections of his own youth. He does not enter into details, but says: "Then we felt that there is a force above both teacher and ourselves—namely, the truth."

Such, then, is what I call the moral element in education provided by the exegetical teaching of the classics. As you see, I am fully justified in calling this subject of instruction moral. Let us now compare with it two other courses of study. I must, however, first beg you to observe that I am giving you again a chapter from the psychological science of knowledges, which is a science not of to-day, but of the future. You will not then ascribe to me a wish to insult or depreciate any branch of study. I must protest most earnestly against any such assumption. I have explained to you before how it was just my own special branch of knowledge which taught me to honour all those other branches also that shoot forth from the majestic tree of Universal Knowledge: I will tell you later how that came about. But, gentlemen, in comparing the horse with the eagle, we surely have the right to say that the eagle has wings and the horse not. Well, does this assertion imply that we depreciate the horse ? The horse has other virtues which the eagle has not. In the same way, in the present question, I do fully recognise not merely the immense importance of mathematics but also its great educational value. None the less, I am justified in saying that we cannot assign to that subject the educational moral force of which I am here speaking. Of course, like classics, it also pursues the truth, but how ? By the process of strict and precise deductions which permit of no scientific dispute. An opinion which does not correspond with the truth is, of course, untenable ; but in mathematics such an opinion cannot even be formed by any reasonable process—at any rate, in the mathematical course prescribed for our secondary schools. This is shown even by its history. Of course, there was a time when no one knew that the sum of the angles in a triangle is equal to two right angles ; or that the sum of two numbers, multiplied by their difference, is equal to the difference of their squares. Once, however, these truths were ascertained, no further dispute on the subject was even possible. Thus mathematics does not teach you to change your opinion on account of the more convincing arguments advanced by your opponent ; it does not call for that important and profitable control over self, which results in the frank confession : "I began by disputing your assertion, but now I see that you were right." And precisely on these grounds we are justified in classing mathematics with those branches of instruction which we may term indifferent for morality, or, in other words, non-moral.

Modern languages, including Russian, form the opposite extreme. These have, of course, to be known; but we are now speaking not of the knowledge itself, but of the way in which this knowledge is attained. And I am sure you know the process well. You use such and such an expression; you are corrected—"that is wrong." Doubtless the people who correct you know their business, and you profit by taking note of their corrections; you will acquire all the more rapidly the knowledge at which you are aiming. But have you yielded to argument? Have you bowed before the force of knowledge or truth? No! Knowledge and truth have no place here; you have bowed before the authority of a person whom you presume rightly enough to possess the learning which you wish to acquire. If a dispute arise, the teacher's word is decisive. Against the verdict "that is right" or "that is wrong" it is useless to argue or raise objections. Now, suppose that this unquestioning acquiescence with the verdict of "right" or "wrong" has passed into your flesh and blood, what, then, will your attitude be toward the various questions which await you in life? A purely dependent attitude is a foregone conclusion. That blessed reflection, "that is right," will be a panacea in every doubtful case. "That is right." Who says so? That is a matter of no importance; whether it be the authorities, or society, or my party, or my associates, or the Press, no matter—the whole difference consists merely in the colour of the livery. And this is why I call such a method of arriving at knowledge unfavourable in regard to educational morality, or, in other words, immoral. And if the teaching of modern languages should be developed in our secondary schools at the expense of instruction in the classics, the result must inevitably be a development of that obstinacy and intoleration which even at present are so rampant in our midst.

Such is, then, the view which weighs the moral element in any given educational course—a new page out of a yet unwritten book dealing with the psychological science of knowledges. It shows us that the method of interpretation applied in classical reading is in the highest degree "educationally moral," since it admits of differences of opinion and decides them by the authority of the truth. Our method is of value, apart from all other considerations, merely because it produces in the learner the habit of yielding to persuasion; that is to say, the capacity of taking newly ascertained facts into consideration and recognising their cogency as arguments. And it is precisely this capacity for being persuaded which is the indispensable condition for a profitable dispute and a reasonable agreement.

I have been insisting hitherto on the educationally moral side of instruction in classical literature.

There is, however, another side which I may call the educationally intellectual. And, in fact, in the example which I gave you, what was the cause of my mistake? Insufficient observation. And what was the cause of my change of opinion? An addition to the materials for observation. Thus, if we ask ourselves how to define our method of exegetical interpretation, we must answer: "An empirical method of observation, as contrasted with the deductive method of mathematics on the one hand, and the experimental method of physics and kindred sciences on the other." Judged from this point of view, no sciences except the Natural Sciences, in the strict sense of the word, can compare with a careful reading of the classics, and even these only if the field of observation be thrown open to the scholar in its fullest extent. Suppose that I send a boy to a willow plantation to determine the nature of a willow, whether it is monœcious or diœcious; in this case the field of observation does mean something, since there are many trees, and he can both make and correct mistakes. But you will easily see that we cannot bring the willow grove into school. No, the only material for the empirical method of observation possible in a class-room is classical reading. It alone puts at the scholar's disposal the whole field of observation—namely, the text. And the boy's intelligence trained by this method will be prepared for its tasks not merely in the field of the Natural Sciences, but in the field of real life. In the affairs of life deduction plays a small part, experiment a smaller part still. Experience in life is gained almost entirely by observation and the proper actions taken in connection therewith.

These are the two sides of classical instruction regarded as an educational method. We now pass to the actual books read, and I must first of all lay stress on the intellectual character of classical literature as well as that of the languages. I have already insisted on the latter point and contrasted it with the sensuous character of modern languages. Now, classical literature, as the product of the classical languages, bears the same stamp as they do. The recognition of the supremacy of reason permeates it throughout its whole extent. As the Greek word πείθομαι means both "I let myself be convinced" and "I obey," just so in Greek literature and its pupil, Roman literature, we meet everywhere a uniform atmosphere, if I may use the expression, a diffused consciousness that *Will* is directed by *Reason*. We often, indeed, hear the view expressed by persons, who believe themselves classical scholars, that the ancient world bowed before fate. But the fact is that a very great amount of knowledge is needed to form a correct judgment regarding Antiquity. The classical peoples were, to employ a happy expression of Vladimir Solovioff's, not single-thoughted, but many-thoughted. Bearing in mind this relation of reason to will, we might compare the evolution of the world's literature to a ballistic curve which returns to the plane whence it started. Its beginning is the most primitive literature in which man's doings are explained by the supposition that he is possessed by good or evil spirits. As late as Homer we find traces of this idea, though he makes efforts to free himself from its influence. Æschylus triumphantly presents us with the principle of unlimited freewill actuated by reason. This principle is the basis of all the succeeding philosophy and literature of the ancient world; it may fairly be counted the culminating point of our curve. As the moderns began to appear on the scene, emotion began to master intelligence. Classicism was challenged by the Romantic movement and its descendants, which, though they might bear different names, still bore one hallmark of identity—the supremacy of Will over Reason. The furthest advances in this direction have been made by modern Russian literature, especially by Dostoyevski. His writings form the furthest point as yet reached; the curve has returned to the plane of its starting-point. Mankind is once again guided by good and bad spirits under the names of passions and inspirations. All this is consummate art in its way, but not from the educational point of view, for it is profitable for a man, while still in the stage of development, to recognise the sway of reason, even though in later life he should come to see that his neighbours are guided not by reason and grounded conviction, but by passion and caprice.

I now proceed. The classical authors not merely took extraordinary pains in regard to style; they stood at the acme of the culture of their time, and they might readily have applied to themselves Lassalle's proud dictum: "I write each one of my words armed in the panoply of the culture of my age." That ancient culture, though far less profound than ours in special branches of knowledge, was yet far more many-sided in the mind of each of its great representatives. All attempts at understanding the classical authors should take account of this fact. And hence we are not without reason for saying that the science of Antiquity is not a special science in the sense in which the term is used of the other sciences, which are wrapped up in their own self-sufficiency. It is rather an encyclopædic course, which brings its exponents continually into touch with other departments of knowledge. It maintains and fosters a consciousness of the unity of knowledge and a respect for all its various branches. Thanks to all this process, it discloses to the view a larger horizon than any special branch of science can reveal. "A classic can make use of everything," "Ein Philologe kann alles brauchen," was a favourite maxim of my lamented teacher Ribbeck, who was himself one of the most highly educated and enlightened men of his time. A classical teacher finds himself bound to summon to his aid at every step now jurisprudence, now an acquaintance with naval and military matters, now political and social sciences, now psychology and æsthetics, now natural science and anthropology, now, again —and this is the most common case of all—experience in life. It is obvious that it is just such a master who is most likely to be a real teacher of his pupils. He is the very one to influence their whole mind, the very one, as an all-sided man himself, to educate a man in that age when the mind is still all-sided and has not yet made a speciality of any science. Hence it may be gathered how limited an acquaintance with the classical school those people possess who reproach it with deciding the choice of a man's special study when he is still a child. The truth is just the opposite: it is precisely classical education which leaves the fullest freedom of choice right up to the highest classes. In support of these remarks I will permit myself to cite a few examples. Whoever cares to multiply them will find a rich harvest in that admirable book, Cauer's "Palæstra Vitæ."

In the Œdipus Rex, Sophocles describes the season of the summer pasturage in these words: "From the spring till Arcturus" (line 1137). The latter reference is quite obscure; my scientific conscience forbids me to remain content with the mere translation. I begin by satisfying myself as to whether my pupil knows what Arcturus is; or, rather, I satisfy myself that he is completely innocent of any idea about it whatsoever. And that is a pity, for it is shameful to see in the starry heavens nothing but a mass of glittering dots. I shall point out to him this glorious bright star on the map and show him how to find it in reality. But that is not enough. What is the meaning of "till Arcturus"? I must explain to him what is meant by the morning rising of a star or constellation, and for this purpose I must first take measures to understand it myself. Even then the matter is not ended. Why does the poet have recourse to such a complicated definition of time? The morning rising of Arcturus occurs about the 10th of September. Why, then, does the poet not say "till September," or rather, as he was an Athenian, "till Boëdromion"? I must explain to the boy that in Sophocles' time the different Greek states had all calendars of their own. It would have been ridiculous, therefore, if a Sophoclean character, who was a Corinthian, started to use the terms of the Athenian calendar. Yet if he used the Corinthian words he might not have been understood. The poet was, therefore, forced involuntarily to have recourse to the calendar common alike to all Greece and to all humanity—the astronomical calendar. . . . And yet altogether involuntarily? No, voluntarily as well. I will endeavour to make my pupil realise the charm of that epoch when the starry heavens still said so much to mortals, when men noted all their changes and arranged by them the time of yearly labour and the time of night watches and guided their vessels by the stars, when the knowledge of their eternal order uplifted man's mind to a hopeful surmise of the everlasting Cause which is revealed in them.

Let me take another example—this time from the same poet's Electra. Clytemnestra, who had murdered her husband, has been visited by a terrible dream; her daughter Electra and the younger woman's companions have no doubt that this vision was sent by the angry shade of her murdered lord Agamemnon, and that consequently the hour of vengeance is nigh. "Take heart, child," they say to her. "Surely your sire, the Prince of Hellas, is mindful: mindful, too, is that ancient two-edged axe which slew him then ruthlessly!" (*v.* 483). Are we to count this merely a poetical fancy? No; we feel ourselves transported into the ideas and beliefs of a primitive period. Anthropology alone is capable of illuminating for us the mental outlook which inspired these ideas and these feelings. The spirit of the murdered king, wroth amid the shades of the underworld and demanding vengeance—this is no creation of a poet's fancy; it is a real object of popular belief. The dead man actually sent that terrible vision to his unfaithful wife. And he could do it, moreover, for that murky habitation, whither she sent him down before his day, was deemed also to be the home of dreams; here they repose by day like bats under the vaulted roof of a cave, and from here they take their flight as the darkness falls. But the idea concerning the axe is of peculiar significance. As we see, it, too, is endowed with feelings. It takes part in the deed, and burns with the wish to atone for the first unrighteous murder by a second righteous and necessary one. Not till that be accomplished will the spirit of the curse which dwells in the axe be satisfied. We find ourselves here in the presence of a so-called "object-soul," a relic of primitive animism. That conception gave rise in early times to an actual jurisdiction over material objects, and even now it is not absolutely dead. "Yes," you may ask, "but why transport ourselves into these primitive and savage ages?" Well, in the first place that we should perceive that they are not savage and that we should not share the intolerable conceit of "up-to-date" gentlemen, but mainly because they were the cradle of many of those moral and judicial ideas on which we draw even to the present day.

I will cite yet another example, which is particularly interesting as affording material for a comparison between ancient and modern poetry. In the tenth book of the Odyssey (line 510) there occurs the description of a place lying on the further side of Ocean, the portal to the realm of shades. And a gloomy picture it is:

> *ἔνθ' ἀκτή τε λάχεια καὶ ἄλσεα Περσεφονείης*
> *μακραί τ' αἴγειροι καὶ ἰτέαι ὠλεσίκαρποι.*

"There are a lowly strand and sacred groves of Persephone, lofty poplars and willows, which lose (or, destroy) their fruits." Why have the poplars and willows received this epithet, which at first sight seems so strange? An epithet, be it noted, which is far more poetical in the Greek than in the translation, owing to its being there but a single word. Well, the connection of thought is as follows. The poplar and the willow both belong to what are called the diœcious class of trees; that is to say, some of them give only masculine flowers, whereas the others give only feminine flowers. There are no trees in these classes of both masculine and feminine type, like the oak and the great majority of other trees, which are therefore called monœcious. If, then, poplars and willows stand singly or in groups of individuals of one sex only, they cannot produce descendants; they "lose their fruits." Of course, Homer did not know the process of the fructification of trees; hence it comes that he employs here the word "fruits" in place of "the unfertilised flowers." The phenomenon itself, however, of the loss of the "fruits" was remarked equally by himself and by his hearers, and that is the reason why he has furnished his unfruitful realm of shades with precisely willows and poplars. The object itself and its beautiful epithet both possess in this case a deep symbolical, in other words a poetical, significance. Now allow me to contrast with the king of Greek poets the king of modern Russian poets—namely, Pushkin. I will recall to your minds the fine poem in which he describes the impression made upon him after a long absence by his home. "Again I trod that corner of the earth," and so on. In the course of the poem we meet the following passage:

On the edge
Of my ancestral lands, just where the road
Rain-stabb'd and scarr'd winds up the hill, there stand
Three pine-trees, one apart, the other twain
Close by each other. Here in moonlit nights,

As I rode by, the rustle of their tops
Would ever greet me with familiar sound.
By this path now I drove, and spied again
The trees before me, still the same as ever:
Again their rustling music, so well known,
Fell on my ear. But round their hoary roots,
Where erstwhile all was waste and barren ground,
A young grove now has sprung and clusters thick
Like children 'neath their shadow. But apart
And gloomy their companion stands, alone
Like an old unwedded man, and round him now
All is as empty as before!

Now, regarded as poetry, this picture is flawless; it would be perfection in every respect if the poet had only chosen with Homer willows or poplars instead of pines. The pine tree is monœcious, and under no circumstances can be regarded as an unwedded bachelor. The process which the poet's fancy has described here does not correspond with reality. Does this imply that we must depreciate Pushkin's merit as a poet? Far from it. The poet is not expected to be omniscient; ignorance of botany does not prevent him from fulfilling his chief duty, which is "to arouse noble feelings in men's hearts." But still the fact remains that the poetry of Homer and of the ancients generally gains if looked at by the eyes of the student of nature; the poetry of Pushkin and, generally speaking, of the moderns loses thereby.* But is it not a sin, you may ask, to destroy the effect of a fine passage of poetry by petty botanical objections? Yes, it is, indeed; there I quite agree with you. That is to say, in other words, it is a sin to

* This cannot be said of Tennyson.

employ modern poetry for exegetical reading—another proof of the correctness of Wundt's theory that the application of the method employed in classical reading to modern authors must inevitably result in mere petty criticism ("Logic," ii. 2, § 314). The poetry of the ancients has been frequently compared with Nature; the comparison is justified in the feature which we are at present discussing, as in many others. Like Nature, it is whole and shrinks from no responsibility; modern poetry is quite another thing. If you possess a ring which is a masterpiece of jeweller's work, you may admire it as much as you please, but only while you look at it with the naked eye; otherwise you find so many defects in it that you will lose all your pleasure in regarding it. But a tiny rose-leaf or a butterfly's little wing—these you can examine as critically as you choose, even with a microscope, and each fresh examination will reveal new and interesting features for your instruction.

I have purposely chosen passages for the explanation of which the classic is obliged to turn for help to sciences comparatively unconnected with his own subject. From these examples you can easily imagine what interesting and varied topics present themselves in the departments of knowledge more closely allied and akin to classical scholarship, such as history and æsthetics. I must here remark that in this particular respect Greek literature stands higher in almost all relations than the literature of Rome; just as the Greek authors studied in our schools stand, generally speaking, on a higher level than the Roman. The champions of classical education, who see the centre of gravity in the study of the ancient languages as such, can content themselves in some measure with the retention of Latin alone. But those who set special store by the ancient literatures must naturally desire the retention of Greek as well. We must suppose, of course, that they know what exactly they want. Further, every one will agree with me, I suppose, that such comments on the text as I have offered above will be in place only if the passage read presents no great difficulties of grammar or syntax. If I am obliged to engage in mutual effort with my pupils in order to establish the form of ἄλσεα, or the verb from which ὠλεσίκαρπος is derived, and so on, we should have no time for deeper and more interesting questions. And so the proposal to defer the beginning of the study of the classical languages as such till the pupil has entered the middle classes would simply postpone the drill in grammar from the middle classes, where it is at present discontinued, to the higher classes. Such a system would compel us to sacrifice exactly those elements of classical education which its advocates themselves are the first to recognise as the most desirable and useful. If I am asked to force an orange into a cup too small for it, I can certainly manage to do so; I have only to squeeze it, but in the process the juice will escape and the unpalatable parts alone remain.

But to return to my theme. In my previous

lectures I have already referred to the historical spirit imparted by classical study as an important asset in education. To-day, too, I touched on this subject in connection with classical semasiology,* but it comes out still more clearly in the course of reading. The commune in Homer, the Greek states at the epoch of the Persian wars described by Herodotus, the Athens of the time of Demosthenes, the development of the Roman Republic in Livy, its fall in Cicero, the rise of the principate in Horace—that is the political background presented to the young scholar's gaze, and to it he should continually turn his eyes in the course of his literary study. Even in this connection the principle of evolution may be explained and grasped. One may see how it involves certain elements of culture and morals; while others triumphantly defy its assaults and maintain their position unshaken to the end. Homer's commune has passed away; but Hector's love for Andromache has never become an anachronism.

And, taken all in all, these successive epochs of Antiquity do, indeed, form a common background, almost equidistant from our own times. In studying it we recognise a common starting-point for all the ideas which mould us to-day. In this connection the moral judgment which we may pass on the phenomena and ideas of Antiquity, valuable as it may be, cannot affect our appreciation of their great importance. For instance, slavery, as we all know, was a lamentable institution; but

* Cf. page 65.

slavery has passed away, and its passing was due to the assault of those ideas regarding the unity of the human race which were developed by the ancients. The tribunal of public conscience is, on the other hand, a pleasing and noteworthy phenomenon. Now it awakened anew to life, after long eclipse, through the effect of these same ideas which were entertained in Antiquity. And so everywhere. Evil lacks vitality and perishes; good possesses it and survives. This consideration I believe to be at the bottom of that optimism and idealism, that healthy and honest frame of mind, which the study of Antiquity promotes. The fact that classical education does inculcate such an outlook has long been observed. As early as the beginning of last century the well-known German author, J. P. Richter, remarked: "Mankind of to-day would sink into a bottomless abyss, if our youth on their journey to the fair of life did not pass through the tranquil and noble shrine of Antiquity" (Levana).

The impulse here alluded to is closely connected with a second, which has reference to the essential meaning of classical interpretation. Every author worthy of the name writes in such a way that his adult and educated contemporaries can understand him without requiring the assistance of expositors. Explanation of the text, therefore, is justifiable only when the historical background, in the light of which the work in question was by itself intelligible, has become dim for us; the more it has changed, the more acceptable is editorial work. This is why commentaries of the classics stand on such a high level; whereas a similar method applied in schools to modern writers must degenerate, as Wundt remarks, into a discussion of trivialities. This is also one of the reasons—not the only one—why we must approve of the opinion expressed by Goethe in a conversation with Eckermann (vol. iii. 99): "Study not your compeers and fellow-toilers, but great men of old, whose works have retained undiminished respect and value for centuries . . . study Molière, Shakespeare, but always and before all the ancient Greeks."

I will now touch on one further point, my last. There is one feeling that is precious for every man, a feeling which school training and it alone can inculcate; I refer to the feeling for truth in the wide sense of the term. Taken in its narrow sense, it simply means that no one should wilfully misrepresent in speaking the picture impressed on his memory by his senses and his powers of reflection; that is to say, should lie. In the wide sense, however, it includes the demand that this picture should correspond as nearly as possible with reality. The first condition apart from the second is almost useless. What would be the good of a photographer's refusing to touch up his work if his faulty camera turns out mere caricatures? Now, it is just the second, the main feeling for truth, that the school should develop, for the task is beyond the power of the family. In the family circle a boy is continually hearing hastily formed judgments, dictated by sympathy or antipathy; he grows accustomed to train his own judgment in the same easy-going fashion. The school, and the school alone, can teach him how to work that his judgments should conform to truth. Now, the most necessary condition for this capacity is that a man should take his knowledge not at third or tenth hand, but at first hand only. And in this respect our exegetical reading takes a foremost place. Every other branch of knowledge comes to a boy at third or tenth hand; ancient culture alone is learnt at first hand. As he reads Herodotus and Livy he peruses at the same time the first-hand authorities for Greek and Roman history—the same as those used by Grote and Mommsen. We can easily understand how much the educational value of Antiquity would lose if the originals should come to be replaced by translations. I do not refer here to our debarring our pupils from the original authorities and accustoming them to be satisfied with knowledge at second hand; this is bad enough, but this is far from all. The celebrated writer on law, Jhering, drew from a passage of Sophocles a completely erroneous conclusion as to the practice of polygamy in heroic times; he had read it in a translation, whereas the original would have saved him from his mistake. Classical critics did not overlook his blunder, seeing in it, rightly enough, the result of neglecting their maxim: "ad fontes!"

And let me not be told that in any case the classical school cannot give its pupils sufficient knowledge to read the originals. Faulty and defective as this knowledge may be, still it enables a man, if obliged to glance at some ancient author, to check a translation by the original; and in our historical age every worker in research and every writer may find himself in this position. This recalls to my mind the lament of the greatest genius of the Russian people, who had not even this capacity. When his poetic mission directed him to the study of the earliest forms of poetry, he was obliged to read them in the most modern translations. His delicate taste was fully conscious of their shortcomings. "How often do I tear my hair for not having had a classical education!" These are Pushkin's words to Pogodin.*

With these words permit me to close this lecture. What I have said does not, of course, exhaust the characteristics of classical literature. Much has been necessarily omitted; something may be added afterwards in connection with the other elements which compose the mental culture of the ancients—their religion, their art, their philosophy. But it must remain over till my succeeding lectures.

* Barsukoff, "Life and Works of Pogodin" (vol. iii. 59).

LECTURE V

SO far we have confined ourselves to the narrow circle of studies which I call school Antiquity or school classics. I have tried to explain the educational importance of those subjects which in our classical secondary schools occupy the hours given up to the teaching of the so-called ancient languages. These courses consist, as you will remember, first of the system of the ancient languages as such, the system being treated of in its threefold division of etymology, semasiology, or vocabulary, and syntax; and, secondly, in the literature of both nations, which is studied in the originals during the "class reading" of the various authors. But the importance of Antiquity for contemporary society is far from being confined to school classics. As I said at the outset, I see in Antiquity one of the main forces at work in the culture of European peoples. To establish and define the importance of Antiquity for modern culture—that is the task which awaits us to-day.

But before undertaking it let us cast one last look at our schools and school Antiquity. Have I discussed or developed that theme fully? Most assuredly not. My survey made and makes no claim to exhausting that subject. I wished merely to direct your attention to its most important aspects, or, to express myself more cautiously, to those which seem to me to be most important. A sense of duty, however, bids me consider, even if briefly, certain other aspects which may seem of most importance to others, though I myself purposely omitted them. These are two in number. Emphasising, as I did, the intellectual importance of classical studies, I passed lightly over their moral advantages; and similarly, when I dealt with their educational value, I disregarded almost entirely the utilitarian element which is closely connected with it. We have not time now to remedy this; permit me simply to present more clearly these two aspects.

I omitted the directly moral value of classical studies in education. Others might possibly have sought to put just this aspect prominently forward. They might have reminded you that Antiquity has bequeathed to us immortal pictures of moral nobility and patriotism such as are connected with the names of heroes of history, like Leonidas and Aristides, Fabricius and Regulus, and, above all, like Socrates; or, again, with the characters depicted by the creative imagination of poets, such as Achilles and Antigone, Œdipus and Iphigeneia. I am convinced that I feel all this as strongly as any one; but I did not and still do not want to discuss it. I preferred to dwell exclusively on the intellectual side. Here we were faced by problems which, though not easy, were still capable of solution. But the process of the moral action of Antiquity in this connection is still obscure for me, and I do not see as yet any direction in which to seek light on that subject. Of course, the psychological science of knowledges will try in time to clear up that question also, but this science is still very far away in the future. If, therefore, I omitted to make any reference to this subject, the reason was not that I undervalued its importance, but that I felt my own incompetence to deal with it.

But when we come to the practical utility of classical studies, it is quite another thing. I forbore to touch on this point because I consider it as only of secondary importance. I know that many will not agree with me. Every one who formulates a question of this nature: "What advantage in life do I gain from Latin and Greek?" has in his mind first of all, and indeed exclusively, their utilitarian value. And, of course, in this sense also they are important and might well afford material for at least a whole lecture. But we value our time, and must perforce leave the question of utility on one side. Still, to avoid its counting itself insulted, I shall try to enumerate its various aspects briefly and without descending into particulars. In the first place, then, the knowledge of Latin is a necessary preliminary to a proper mastery of French and of the Romance languages generally; it makes the study of these languages easier and more intelligible. Secondly, it is a necessity for a lawyer in view of the important part which Roman law has played and still continues to play in both the development of modern law and in the legal courses of our universities. In the third place, the knowledge of the two ancient languages is indispensable for the comprehension of the Greek and Latin words which have been assimilated by the languages of all modern civilised peoples, and more especially in regard to scientific terminology, in which it facilitates our apprehension and makes the words intelligible. This applies specially to students of medicine and of natural science. Fourthly, historical and classical students of the future must possess a knowledge of the classical languages, and they themselves in their turn are indispensable to their country. Finally, from considerations of culture, on which I have already touched, the knowledge of Greek is necessary for Russia especially, seeing that her culture is of Byzantine origin.* A Russian engaged without a knowledge of Greek in researches in literature or history is perfectly inconceivable if we try to figure him as an independent and original scholar.

Such, then, are in brief the chief utilitarian considerations in favour of classical study. They might, of course, be established, developed, and illustrated in far greater detail. This were no difficult task, and the result would prove very convincing. But firstly, as I said, we have no time for that; secondly, just because of its comparative ease this

* See Sandys, "History of Classical Scholarship," ch. xxii, Byzantine scholarship from A.D. 529–1000.

task, more than any other in this connection, may be left to each individual for himself; and thirdly, we have already had an opportunity of convincing ourselves that the principle of utility in school education can play but a subordinate and subsidiary part.

But now let us leave the school and school questions. Let us suppose that the pupils, whether on the classical or modern side, have left school and entered real life. They have adopted each his special career and now constitute educated society. Within its circle an exchange of intellectual wares is maintained in which all the members of society participate. The result of this intellectual commerce forms the mental and moral culture of society at any given period. Now comes the question: Does classical study form an element in this culture, and if so, in what does its importance consist?

Before venturing to answer this question, I think it advisable to recall to your memory the corresponding antithesis, the second of the three which I propounded at the outset of these lectures. With regard to classical study as an element of modern culture, I said, the world has largely made up its mind that this study is practically valueless, as it has been superseded long ago by the achievements of modern thought. The expert, on the other hand, will tell you that our intellectual and moral culture has never been so closely bound up with Antiquity, has never stood in more pressing need of it, and never been so qualified to comprehend and assimilate it as at the present day. I remarked also that the first of these two opinions is the result of a misunderstanding. I will now explain to you wherein this misunderstanding lies.

The fact is that many persons are unable to form any other idea of the influence of Antiquity on modern culture than one which presupposes an avowal of the ancient world as a model for the world of to-day. Then they proceed to ask in what respects can Antiquity be regarded as a model for modern culture. And they answer, not without reason, "In none." Can the heathen religion of Antiquity serve as a model or pattern for modern Christianity? Surely not. Can we arrange the government of our states on the analogy of those of Antiquity, say the Athenian Republic or the Roman Empire? No, again. Can our knowledge of Nature and mankind be enriched by an addition of facts known to the ancients and unknown to us? No, or only to an infinitesimal degree. Are we to force modern poetry, architecture, and painting into the narrow limits imposed on these three arts by ancient technique? No. What, then, is the value of Antiquity for modern culture?

Exceedingly great. The fact is that a theory, which sets up *à priori* a model for imitation, is wrong not merely as regards Antiquity, but also quite generally. All of us who cultivate the field of Antiquity in the full consciousness of the importance and value of our work for our contemporaries and descendants—all of us protest unanimously against this view which is fathered upon us. The idea comes sometimes from allies whose zeal outruns their discretion, but more often from ignorant or malicious foes. No, gentlemen, we have no idea of dragging you back into the past: our gaze is directed forwards and not backwards. When the oak sends its roots deep into the earth on which it flourishes, it is not with the wish to grow back into the earth, but because it is from this soil that it draws the strength to rise to heaven beyond all the herbs and trees which draw their strength merely from the surface. So Antiquity should be not a model, but a source of quickening strength for modern culture.

This point of view enables us to understand the fact that the human mind has never been so well qualified for appreciating and assimilating the lessons of Antiquity as at the present moment. This statement needs, indeed, a corresponding supplement—namely, that the lessons of Antiquity have never been so qualified for being appreciated and assimilated by the human mind as now. The supplementary clause, however, applies not so much to Antiquity itself as to the "science of Antiquity," and consideration of this science must, in accordance with our programme, be postponed to the last lecture. There was a time when people were ignorant of the history of their own country and took no interest in it. "You find all that you need in ancient history," wrote Mably, an eminent man of the period preceding the French Revolution. "You need not study modern history, in which, in any case, you will find nothing but silly and undigested statements." At that particular period people looked to Antiquity to provide them with models for the present. But then the historical instinct awoke; the study of the history of the mother country drew men from the study of ancient history, but it lent to ancient history a new and hitherto unsuspected importance. It dawned upon men that the history of the civilisation of each one of the modern nations formed a tiny rivulet, until Antiquity discharged its broad flood into it, bearing on its current all the ideas, including Christianity, which feed our mind at the present day. Thus, if we adopt the historical attitude, we see that each one of us owns two mother countries: one the native land after which we call ourselves, the other Antiquity. To express this idea in a short formula, allow me to borrow the terms of the Greek theologians, who distinguished three component parts in a man: his body, soul, and spirit—σῶμα, ψυχή, πνεῦμα—and to lay this down: our mother country, as regards our body and soul, is Russia for the Russians, Germany for the Germans, France for the French; but our spiritual mother country is for one and all—Antiquity. The link which connects and unites all European nations independently of their national and racial differences is their common descent from Antiquity. We think alike; and hence we understand each other, whereas the nations who do not belong to the circle of European culture understand neither each other nor ourselves.*

And this fact has already passed into the consciousness of the various nations, though still in a vastly insufficient measure. They are beginning more and more to recognise in Antiquity a common mother country. Italy and Greece are almost holy lands for all of us. The civilised nations of Europe try as hard as each can to secure some corner of these countries for purposes of research and excavation. Every discovery of any importance in ancient art and literature engages the interest of the whole civilised world; whereas similar discoveries in modern literature and art seldom raise any emotion beyond the limits of the countries which they may chance to concern directly. Yes, Antiquity, the common mother country, is the foundation of the unity of European civilisation, and hence the centripetal forces of European culture, on the other hand, also tend directly or indirectly to the advantage of classical study. This position of affairs has important bearings on the attitude towards Antiquity assumed by the two parties into which society is divided in the countries of European culture, the "Nationalists" and the "Europeanists," or, as they are called in Russia, the "Slavophils" and the "Occidentals." If a Nationalist adopts a hostile attitude toward

* This argument might be used to throw light on the fact that so much of the Russian spirit and literature, Dostoyevski for example, is half unintelligible to Western Europe.

Antiquity, that shows merely his ignorance: he either is ignorant of or forgets the fact that the study of Antiquity has formed from the very earliest times an element in the culture of his own nation, and that accordingly his scorn of Antiquity dooms him to ignorance of what he, as a Nationalist, would have liked to know. If, however, an Occidental takes the same view, he betrays a still greater ignorance; he is simply sawing off the branch on which he is sitting.

Thus the development of the history of culture among modern nations has shown what a tremendous rôle the common mother country, Antiquity, has played in the formation of their intellectual and spiritual qualities. Is this all there is to say? No, not all. For we might be met by a very simple rejoinder—well, but what is the use of our past? Live in the present! Yes, of course; but here the natural sciences come to the aid of history, and biology refutes that superficial saw: "What has been is no more." No, gentlemen, what has been is. We cannot separate ourselves from our past, for this past lives in ourselves, just as the whole past of a hoary oak lives in it still, beginning with the time when it was a tiny shoot of a year's growth. This is true for every individual, and still more so for societies or nations. We must study our past to know ourselves; are we not the outcome of our past? And we must know ourselves, that we may guide our lives according to reason and not live, like the brute beasts, unconsciously. Now, this learning is not taught at school; it is gained in the course of a man's whole life, for it is the outcome of that same exchange of intellectual wares of which I have already spoken.

Let us, however, proceed to particulars—to the elements of culture bequeathed to us by Antiquity, which we employ as quickening forces on our own culture.

Of these elements religion, of course, takes the foremost place. Antiquity, however, has bequeathed to us not one, but two religions—the Christian and the heathen, the latter being the religion of Antiquity in its narrow sense. As a matter of fact, we cannot separate the idea of Christianity from that of classical culture. In the first place—though this is not the main reason—because Greek is the language of the oldest Christian writings, and language is, as we have seen already, the confession of a people. Yes, Christianity in the form in which it has come down to us drew strength from the Greek people, as the oak from the soil. We cannot understand Christianity without studying its Greek records. Let us take, for instance, the injunction about non-resistance to evil which has become so famous in Russia.* Did the Saviour really teach us not to resist evil, or merely not to resist with evil? It is not my business to try to decide that dispute.

* The cardinal point in the Tolstoyan doctrine. No English writer has combated it with such philosophic breadth and acuteness as the Russian thinker Vladimir Solovioff.

I would only direct your attention to this fact—namely, that to come to a decision you must depend not on a Slavonic or Russian translation, but, of course, on the Greek original. Now, it happens that the Greek text is, indeed, somewhat dubious. In the phrase μὴ ἀντιστῆναι τῷ πονηρῷ the word πονηρῷ is grammatically capable of meaning either "against evil" or "with evil." You will remember, if any of you have read Lieskovski's "Kolivanski mujz," the great theological discovery which the baron communicated to his nephew, the hero of the book—namely, that in the Lord's prayer the true reading is not our *nasuschtchniy* (daily) bread, but *nadsuschtchniy*, that is to say, spiritual. Such, he urged, was the meaning of the Greek ἐπιούσιος· The poor hero, in his bewilderment, is quite at a loss for an answer. Had he known Greek, however, he might easily have refuted his uncle's heresy by showing that *nadsuschtchniy* would have been in Greek ὑπερούσιος, or rather, perhaps, ὑπερουσιακός, and could not have been ἐπιούσιος. These instances may show the importance of Greek for an educated Christian. I have noticed them, however, merely incidentally : our real purpose is different.

I connected Christianity with Antiquity not only because Greek was the language of original Christianity, but chiefly because the two are connected by their common development and spirit. Christianity was, of course, the complement of the Hebraic law and the Old Testament prophecies ; but it was also the complement in at least an equal degree of the immemorial struggles and aspirations of the nations of Antiquity. This fact was not appreciated by former critics, and hence the second religion, the religion of Antiquity in its narrow sense, was deemed useless and, indeed, harmful. In the present day, however, it is fairly well known and carefully studied. We bow before the sublime conceptions of this religion of the ancient heathens. We read with genuine reverence the prayer to Zeus in Æschylus—I cited a passage from it in a former lecture—in which the chorus thank God "whoever he may be, for that he has directed mankind to the way of knowledge by putting into force the maxim: 'Learn by suffering.' And lo! in the night season comes in place of sleep unsleeping care and pulses at our hearts with never-ceasing drops, and even against our wills we learn to be righteous. Such is the grace (χάρις) granted to mankind by God, who sits in his might at the sacred rudder of the universe."

As you see, I make a distinction between the religion and the mythology of the ancients, which were formerly regarded as identical. Of course, there are certain myths which are the bearers of religious doctrines as well. But the majority of these myths have for us, as they had for the ancients, only an æsthetic or ethical interest. What is to be said about this ancient or, to speak more correctly, this Greek mythology? Would that I had the gift of our great national poet to describe that mythological world to you in colours of life and reality, the rustle of the evergreen oak of Greek saga, that grew in the oldest of Greek sanctuaries, the storm-encircled Dodona ! * What a treasure-house of marvellous pictures ! There wrathful Achilles gazes with beating heart on his countrymen's blazing ships, a satisfaction to his wounded dignity ; there old King Priam, to ransom his son's corpse, kisses meekly the slayer's hand ; there Odysseus, long-suffering wanderer, wearies for his distant land and prizes not a goddess' favours ; there bold Jason musters his hero-band for the wondrous raid into golden Colchis ; there faithful Orpheus descends into the abode of death to beg his Eurydice from the Queen of Shades. There we see the proud martyr Antigone bartering her life for the privilege of paying a debt of love to her dead brother ; there the gentle Iphigeneia submitting willingly to death for her father's glory ; there jealous Medea slaughtering her children in the madness of her revenge ; there the stone effigy of the once blessed Niobe weeping over her shattered happiness.

These figures have never perished. They captivated the greatest spirits of Antiquity, as long as that Antiquity had life. After its death they were taken over by the Middle Ages to receive a new lease of life, partly with the same names, partly with new titles. Venus, the Queen of Beauty, entices knights into her magic grotto ; the stout

* A reference to Pushkin's "Ruslam and Ludmilla," which deals with personages of Russian mythology. Glinka's famous opera is founded on this poem.

mariner Odysseus sails far over the ocean till his bark founders on the perpendicular rock of Purgatory; Circe, the sorceress, under the name of Armida, seeks to hold back the Crusaders from their sacred exploits; Helen leaves the Greek heroes for the heroic thoughts of Faust. And ever richer grows the wreath of poetry that encircles the brow of the Greek legendary figures. Each succeeding epoch of modern times has added to it new blossoms. Achilles and Œdipus, Antigone and Medea—these are no longer Greek figures; the love of humanity as a whole has adopted them.

And, as belonging to humanity, they have come down to us and to-day are ours, the most glorious inheritance bequeathed to us by our spiritual country. And our spirits unite with them not merely to our pleasure but to our instruction. These figures, after passing through the furnace of the world's history, have lost the fleeting, transitory, and we might almost say earthly, character which stamped them at the beginning; they have now become but embodiments of ideas, of inestimable value to the poet-thinker. And not merely to him. I have said already that these figures unite with the creations of modern times and live on in our own day, though under changed names. The hapless Orestes, oppressed with the duty of blood vengeance, survives on our stage in the person of the Danish prince Hamlet; but this is only the smallest fraction of the whole. How many high-spirited female martyrs owe their origin to Antigone! How many brooding plotters to Medea! Even their creators are often ignorant of this fact, and imagine that they are hearkening to the voice of their own soul. They do not know that this voice is still the same rustle of the evergreen oak of Greek legend, that grew in the sacred grove of Pelasgic Zeus in storm-encircled Dodona.

Mythology forms the contents of an important part of ancient poetry, and so leads us by a natural process from the religion of the ancients to their literature. Ancient literature, however, concerns us not merely on account of its contents, but on account of its form and, above all, of its spirit. With regard to its form, I beg you to remember that the ancient classics have created all the various types vital to modern literature. I mean literally created, for they did not exist previously; and created them, moreover, not by one sudden effort but in due succession and in an orderly process of organic development.

And here I would like to ask every one who is interested in literature—and who is not nowadays? —what are his views respecting these types of literature of unknown origin which he meets in his life. Why do we possess precisely these types—tragedy, comedy, novels, tales, lyric poetry, epigrams, and so on—and not other types? Why are rhyme and metre indispensable for some kinds of literature and metre only for others, whereas others again need neither rhyme nor metre? What, I repeat, are the views of any one interested in literature when confronted with these facts?

Well, I suppose, most people, if they were to answer honestly, would say: "We have none." And it is true that whoever lives only in the present soon loses the habit of thought, for thought implies the connecting cause and effect, and the cause of the present lies in the past. But let us take a thoughtful person. If he is anxious to explain the reason, he will probably turn to the science of literature, the theory of writing. He will speedily be undeceived. The theory of literature, regarded as a science, is reserved for the future; at present it classifies and illustrates rather than explains. No. For a reflective person there is at present only one path available. The question as to the sense of the different types of literature can be answered only by the history of their origin and development—that is to say, by ancient literature.

In this field we are able to see clearly how the lyrical-epic primitive germ gives rise to, first of all, epic poetry. As writing had not been invented, memory was the only storehouse for all the stock of man's necessary knowledge, and metre and melody had to be called in as memory's handmaids. Thus the whole circle of man's necessary knowledge began to be embodied in the epos—the exploits of the gods and of ancestors, prophecies, laws, exhortations regarding life and work. Hence it was that epic poetry parted into two branches—the heroic and the didactic. The development of music led to the complication of metres; from the epos developed lyrical poetry with all its various branches—elegy, ballad poetry, the lay, the ode. Lyrical poetry spread its influence ever wider and wider, until at last it absorbed the epos and produced in common with it the drama, tragedy, and comedy. But at the same time the art of writing was becoming more and more common. The result is prose. Prose now competes with poetry as the storehouse of indispensable knowledge. It is still felt, however, that poetry commands advantages denied to prose; its metrical character corresponds more closely with the emotional moods of the human soul than the even flow of its rival. So poetry continues to express the emotional and passionate side of human nature, leaving the intellectual side to prose. Epic poetry passes away, historical and philosophical prose take its place. But life assumes ever new developments; the law-courts are the scene of as furious passions as the popular assemblies. Thus there arises a new branch of prose which finds room for passion—namely, the oratorical. Through this element of passion oratorical prose draws near to poetry. It adopts a kind of metre which is called prose rhythm. It turns its attention to the harmonious division of its periods, and here and there, when it wishes to leave a stronger impression than usual, it marks these divisions by rhyme.—With this lyrical element oratorical prose threatened poetry with extinction, but this calamity was postponed thanks to the love which the Greeks cherished for their past after their loss of political independence.

Then came the rise of the romantic poetry of the so-called Alexandrian period. This poetry recalled to life the earlier types of poetry, and added to them that hitherto unknown genuine expression of the romantic mood, the idyll. Meantime literature had found its way to Rome. This migration also led to the reappearance of discarded types of poetry, though now in the Latin language, and to the creation of a new type, the natural product of the contact of an exotic culture and native barbarism—namely, the Roman satire.—But, in spite of all, the triumph of prose over poetry was merely postponed. Fully conscious of its strength, prose forced its way from the world of reality into the domain of imagination, which had hitherto been reserved for poetry. The result was the novel and the tale, the latest offspring of classical literature.—Another circumstance also led to the triumph of prose. In the first Christian epoch the quantitative value of syllables, which had been characteristic of the ancient languages, and on which the whole system of ancient scansion depends, began to be abandoned. Thus, when a new form of popular poetry was called for, owing to various causes, among them being the influence of Christianity, the form of the new type of poetry was borrowed partly from ancient poetry but mainly from rhythmical prose. The characteristic property of the latter, the harmonious division, marked by rhyme, of its periods, now became the characteristic feature of this new poetry also. And thus arose a late classical poetry which lasted all through the Middle Ages: "Stabat mater dolorosa Iuxta crucem lacrimosa," and all the rest.* And this is precisely the form of poetry which has conquered all the nations of European culture and has expelled the rude native forms which were incapable of development. We, the nations of modern Europe, all share in this legacy, and the remark applies to even our popular poetry.—It is true that many attempts have been made to replace these ancient forms of poetry by others borrowed from the poetry of other than the classical peoples, such as the Hindoos or the Arabs; but all such attempts have proved failures. And what is more, our neighbours the Germans have never succeeded in even resuscitating their immemorial type of poetry, the alliterative. Sometimes, indeed, it has been imitated with great success, especially by Wagner in his famous trilogy, "Helle Wehr, Heilige Waffe, Hilf meinem ewigen Eide!" None the less, its horizon is extremely narrow. Its use is impossible beyond the circle of German sagas; neither Faust nor the Jungfrau von Orléans could have been written in that form.

Thus, as regards types and forms, we draw on ancient literature right down to the present day.

* Even in classical times a liking for rhyme manifested itself, as frequently in Ovid, e.g. "Quot caelum stellas tot habet tua Roma puellas." Distinct traces of the adoption of rhyme are to be seen as early as the hymns of Hilary of Poictiers (died 367), and the system attained its highest development in the twelfth and thirteenth centuries. See Chambers's Encyclopædia, *s.v.* Rhyme.

Modern writers have in some ways simplified them, in others complicated them, but have added to them nothing essentially new. I spoke, however, of the spirit of ancient literature as well as its forms, and you doubtless guess for yourselves that it is this spirit which is the most important inheritance bequeathed to us by Antiquity. Yes, indeed. Only I must study brevity here more than anywhere, even at the risk of omitting some very important aspects of my theme. I must content myself with citing two examples. I refer to the spirit of ancient history and the spirit of ancient philosophy, both of which we will consider, of course, only as types of literature.

Historical composition was practised by others besides the two classical nations. The peoples of the East and the Hebrews cultivated it as well. But in the hands of Oriental nations it served quite a special aim — namely, the glorification of the exploits, victories, and buildings of their rulers; their defeats and disgraces were never chronicled. The mainspring of Jewish history was another purpose—to testify to the unremitting care of the God of Sabaoth, who rewarded His chosen people when they kept His commandments and punished them when they disobeyed. Its aim was to trace wherever possible the finger of God. It is among the ancient Greeks that we first find the conception of historical truth. This simply as such would have seemed unmeaning to the historians of the East and of Israel also. Why does Herodotus write his history? "In order that the memory of the deeds of mankind should not perish, and that the great and marvellous achievements alike of Hellenes and Barbarians should not lose their renown." Mark, Barbarians as well as Hellenes! The historian stands above all nationality. It is, indeed, nobility as such which interests him, which claims its due reward from him and receives it quite independently of the performer's race. Of course, every detail in Herodotus is not correct. Mythical stories are told, but with a good-natured *naïveté* and no evil intention. How could he, indeed, not tell them? In his time historical criticism was just in its infancy. Historical criticism! . . . And there I have touched on the next aspect of the case. When I spoke in my last lecture of the feeling for truth, I pointed out to you that this feeling embraced two separate demands: firstly, "See that your words correspond with your judgment," that is to say, "Speak the truth"; secondly, "See that your judgment corresponds with the truth," that is, "Do not make mistakes." Now, the first demand Herodotus satisfied. It was reserved for his successor, Thucydides, to satisfy the second. He is not content with the mere correct reproduction of what he has heard. He endeavours in every possible way to test it. He compares the assertions of the Athenians with those of the Spartans, the Corinthians, and so on. In this way he hopes to arrive at historical truth. Such is his method of verifying his facts. Still, this is in itself a comparatively easy proceeding. The historian is, however, not merely a narrator, but also a judge. And how does Thucydides deliver his historical judgments? In a way in which we could not hope for an improvement. When he is confronted with two opposed and irreconcilable points of view, he develops first one and then the other in the form of disputations held between the representatives of both sides. Speeches certainly occur in Herodotus, but with him they serve merely to enliven agreeably his narrative. With Thucydides they serve to promote the main end of his work—namely, the manifestation of historical truth. Not all his successors, of course, followed his example. In the fourth century we meet with attempts to subordinate historical accuracy to patriotism and mere interest of narrative; but in serious historical writing the great principle of Thucydides' work remained unimpaired. In the second century Polybius wrote the remarkable words which he followed in practice: "Truth is the eye of history" (i. 14). In the first century B.C. Cicero summed up neatly the chief claims to be made on history as follows: "Ne quid falsi audeat, ne quid veri non audeat historia," words which still figure as a motto on the title-page of the most serious historical journal of our age, the French "Revue historique." A hundred and fifty years later Tacitus repeated approximately the same claim with his famous "Sine ira et studio."

Such is the spirit of ancient historical writing. Well, are we now to reproach their method for seeming obsolete to us in this or that respect, for devoting too much attention to foreign politics and too little to economical and social questions? Such criticism would fairly apply, supposing that scholars, such as we claim ourselves to be, wished to recommend the ancient method of writing history as a model for the present day. I have, however, already protested against any such insinuation, and I do so again. No! Antiquity should be considered not as a model, but as a seed plot. We should take and plant this seed of historical truth in our own soil that it might grow into a tree of true historical composition in modern times. It was this point of view which led one of the greatest historians of our age, Ranke, to style himself a pupil of Thucydides.

And it is my firm belief that we have never needed this seed so strongly as to-day. To-day, more than ever before, historical truth, that eye of history, as Polybius called it, is threatened with danger from its two sworn foes, nationalism on the one hand and party spirit on the other. The import of this it is not hard to understand. I do not know whether you are all aware of what some writers mean by "Hottentot morality." The phrase was originated by an ancedote which is perhaps not very credible. A Hottentot was asked by a missionary what was the difference between good and evil. "If my neighbour steals my wife," he answered, "that is evil; if I steal my neighbour's wife, that is good." Now you will understand that this Hottentot principle manifests itself not merely in private relations between individuals—there it is comparatively harmless, and we can afford to laugh at it—but also in the sphere of national and party concerns, where it is far more harmful. Suppose that a Spaniard champions enthusiastically the cause of his fellow-countrymen oppressed in Portugal, but boils with indignation when Portugal, in her turn, protests against the oppression of Portuguese in Spain; suppose, again, that the same Spaniard, as a good Republican, approves of the Government's action in forbidding a Carlist demonstration, but next day abuses the Government for suppressing Republican demonstrations, then he fancies that in all these cases his judgments are fully sound and reasonable. My opinion, on the other hand, is that they are merely Hottentot—in the first case based on national, in the second case on party considerations.

And still I should say that as long as this Hottentot morality affects only our adults in their national and party squabbles, this is by itself not very serious. If I am told that these things are unavoidable, I shall not dispute the statement. But, as you know, our Spaniards are not content with this. They demand that all history, as far as it is written by and for Spaniards, should bear certain corresponding characteristics to show that it was written by a Spaniard and not by a Portuguese. This makes me think sorrowfully of Thucydides. He began his work with the words: "Thucydides, an Athenian, has written this history of the war between the Peloponnesians and the Athenians." And it is fortunate that he did, for without these words, judging simply by the character and tendency of his history, no one could guess of what city the author was, whether Athens or Sparta or Corinth. But what are we to do? History, to maintain its Spanish character, must obviously close her "eye" for all the period covered by modern times. Let us console ourselves, then, with the thought that truth will find a refuge in ancient history at any rate which cannot be written from a Spanish point of view. And, indeed, that fact is a reason for self-congratulations. I would never endorse the saying of Mably, which I quoted, about ancient and modern history. It is, however, beyond doubt that at the present day the study of ancient history is of peculiar moral importance. In estimating it we do not judge on à priori prepossessions. We admire good men and deeds, we are shocked by bad men and deeds, without pausing to enquire after the nation which was responsible for the deeds or doers in question. Our Hottentot ethics have no place here. The more we study ancient history, the more we learn to be just. But this fact is precisely what it does not suit our Spaniards to admit. They demand the elimination of all ancient history from our schools, or at least its reduction in favour of modern history, especially Spanish! . . . You have understood, of course, already that I speak here of Spaniards merely because they live far away and will never find out what I have said about them, and consequently will not feel insulted. Even as it is, in these lectures I have already "insulted" so many people that I need seek no more victims! No; let us return to ourselves. Consider all those claims which are made upon our school instruction in history! It must plant in the pupil's mind the spirit of patriotism, the spirit of this, that, and the next virtues. I fear, however, that nothing profitable will grow up from all this planting, and that in the process the "eye of history" may be irretrievably damaged. No! if it depended on me, I would, as a man nurtured on Antiquity, say modestly but emphatically: "Instruction in history must plant in the pupil's mind the spirit of truth and justice"—and then . . . I would put a full stop.

LECTURE VI

MY preceding lecture I closed with an analysis and characterisation of that which I called the spirit of ancient history writing. I now pass to the spirit of ancient philosophy. I must first warn you, however, that this subject also we will, for the time being, consider not as philosophy, properly speaking, but merely as a type of literature just as we discussed its sister subject.

Let us grant, for a moment, that all the subject-matter of Plato's philosophy is not only untrue, but positively absurd, that it is absolutely valueless for us. Well, are we to stow away his dialogues in musty archives? No! Their importance as works of literature is independent of their philosophical results. What feature in them most strikes a reader who is at all thoughtful? Not their deductions, but the method whereby these deductions are attained. For the sake of clearness let us compare Greek philosophical as well as historical literature with the works which correspond to it among nations uninfluenced by Greek civilisation, the Hindoos, the peoples of the so-called civilised East, the Jews. Among them, also, you find extremely profound doctrines. Nobody can adopt an air of superiority towards the teaching of

Buddha or the Old Testament prophets. But it is among the Greeks that we find a feature which they first introduced into the process of human thought—namely, the conviction which is diffused throughout their philosophy that every position is true as far as it has been proved. Nay, more; it is presupposed that the only criterion for a thinker is whether an argument be proved or not proved, and that once it has been proved beyond doubt, this should form his defence against all the antipathies which the world at large may feel. "How! You assert so and so," Socrates' friend says to him, outraged by his conclusions. "Oh, no!" Socrates answers; "it is not I who make these assertions, but Logos. I am merely its instrument. If you are pleased by what Logos proves through my mouth, so much the better; if displeased, then don't blame me, blame Logos, or still better, yourself."

Now this attitude requires, as a consequence, that you should argue with a man, and argue him over into changing his views. Logos sets us serious, sometimes, indeed, burdensome conditions. You must accept a position, however unpleasant for you, once it is proved; you must reject a conviction, however dear to you, once it is refuted—there is the thinker's code of honour. If you are unwilling to accept it, you will be but a sheep in a flock of sheep, a slave under a master's power, and not a free citizen of the community of spirit. And so refute and prove, but do not complain or abuse your opponent or fly into a passion. And look well after all your arguments, positive and negative, that they be really proved. Very often sympathy or antipathy perverts our judgment and inclines it to accept the most frivolous considerations as valid truths. That should not be. An unproved assertion in argument, suggested by some sympathy, corresponds to an unfair thrust in a duel. Whoever stoops to either breaks the code of honour.

Yes, the change of views under persuasion, that is the seed which ancient philosophy holds in itself, and ancient philosophy alone. And that seed must enter each one of us if we would stand in conscious relations towards the phenomena of life and pass out of the mists of prejudices. Unfortunately, in contemporary mankind, the ground for that seed is very unpromising. We are all of us, according to our inheritance, more or less voluntarists. Intellectualism is only a thin alluvial layer of black earth in the structure of our minds. Our minds may be tuned and tuned again. The conditions and circumstances of our lives influence us fundamentally. But then, all that is the direct opposite of a change of opinion for intellectual reasons.

And now, in discussing this last with you, I am afraid of one thing above all—lest you translate my words into the voluntarist vocabulary and confuse the change of conviction I speak of with what I will permit myself to call vacillation, that infallible sign of moral or mental weakness. The point is not at all that a man should merely change his opinions. That is an everyday phenomenon and not worth mention. At every step, as he passes from one set of conditions to another, a man changes his persuasions, not suddenly, of course, but by degrees. This is true of political persuasion especially. In regard to this sphere of thought such metamorphoses take place with a regularity that falls but little behind the well-known metamorphoses of insects. All round us we see the most radical larvæ turning into the most magnificent reactionary butterflies. You will not suspect me, I trust, of commending metamorphoses of this nature while I refer to change of opinion. No, quite the contrary ; such a process is its direct enemy. And yet not its only enemy. Its other foe is that position which is customarily defined in the voluntarist language by the respectable term stability of conviction, whereas our intellectual phraseology brands it as mental stagnation and obtuseness. From our point of view, as much censure must be attached to the man who, with logically imperative reasons for discarding his opinion, refuses to do so as to the man who abandons his convictions without any logical reasons. Both of them are enemies of and rebels against Logos, that "word-reason," which in the profound phrase of the fourth Gospel was in the very beginning of being, and which was first revealed in ancient philosophy.

Pardon my insistence on this idea. But it has closer bearings on our subject now than ever. At this very moment Logos hovers over all of us, over me who speak to you and over you who listen to me. My words are intended not to move your feelings in this way or that, but to persuade your reasoning faculties. That this task would be difficult, that my lectures would provoke much adverse criticism and dissatisfaction, I knew myself. I told you so at the outset. It is indeed difficult to persuade and induce people to change their opinion in a case where you have to contend with prejudices heaped up during a whole succession of years, transmitted from the society in which those people live, and, one might almost add, bequeathed to them by their ancestors. Nevertheless, I suppose, if it is important for me to communicate to you the truth which I possess, it is no less important for you to receive it . . . as far as it is true. And to convince you there is one means, namely the thinker's code of honour, of which I spoke a moment ago: "You must accept a position, however unpleasant for you, once it is proved; you must reject a conviction, however dear to you, once it is refuted." But unfortunately, among the qualities which distinguish the modern reader and listener from the reader and listener of Antiquity must be included the following characteristic: when you seek to prove anything to him, he lets the course of your arguments flow past his ears or eyes and concentrates all his attention on the conclusion. If that please him—well done! he cries, though the argument itself be never so absurd. If it displease him, anathema! That is the attitude against which I wish to arm you, while there is still time, while I am still in your company.

Yes, I repeat once more, a capacity to change one's opinion for intellectual reasons, that token of mental freedom and mental progress, is the most precious inheritance left to us by ancient philosophy as a literary production. Its corresponding form is the dialogue; and that is the reason why Plato wrote his works in the form of dialogues in which persuasion and change of conviction go on before our eyes.

You understand, of course, that I must necessarily omit many precious aspects of Antiquity, of ancient literature, of ancient philosophical writing. I can show you only small specimens, so to say, and in their choice a certain subjective attitude is inevitable. I speak about what seems to me the most valuable part of the lessons taught us by Antiquity: another man would, perhaps, emphasise other aspects more dear to his heart, and would be just as much right. Now, before parting with ancient literature, I should like once more to indicate its enormous effect on culture throughout history.

If Antiquity had merely created those types of literature which are vital to our own authors, if it were merely the plane of departure for the evolutions of modern writing, then even so its signification would have been very great. Every question as to the causes of phenomena in the literature of all countries, in other words every conscious relation to it, must inevitably lead us into the sphere of Antiquity. But as a matter of fact this does not exhaust its importance. Antiquity not only gave the impulse to modern literatures, but also accompanied them throughout the path of their development and exerted a more or less strong influence upon them. Montesquieu said very truly of his time: "Modern works are written for the reader, ancient for the writer." The classics have been always, and especially in the best periods of literature, the principal source of nourishment for poets and prose writers. To understand modern literature properly a man must have devoted very conscientious study to that source. Former critics were not so alive to that necessity. While historians of literature believed their chief task to be either the collection of facts concerning the external lives of literary men, or moral and æsthetic lucubrations on the subject of their works, it was possible to dispense with a knowledge of ancient literature. But from the time when the history of literature was founded on a scientific basis, and we began to claim from its historian an elucidation of those causes which gave to a certain literary production just a certain character and not some other, from that time the knowledge of ancient literature has become his indispensable duty. For how could he explain the rise of some literary phenomenon if he were ignorant of those forces which produced it? So what I said before is justified in this connection also; the value of the classics has become not less but greater than it was before.

At present, however, it is not that point which is important for us, but rather this next consideration. You will remember that antithesis in which I see the motto of the thinker who insists on the value of Antiquity for the present age. "Not a model," I said, "but a seed." There have been periods in the history of literature when Antiquity was held to be a model for the life of the age. There have been others when it was—not perhaps held to be, but actually was a seed. The first we term imitative. Men imitated what they understood, and they did not understand very much, much less, in fact, than we do now. So the result was not classicism but pseudo-classicism. None the less, these periods were indispensable. They have schooled modern literature, they have communicated to its types and mediums of production that high degree of technical excellence which it needed to ensure its serving higher aims. It is unfortunate that the shortness of time at our disposal does not permit of my developing this most interesting and important subject. But, to pass over that point, we count the really creative periods of literature those when the classics were not so much a model as a seed—it is no matter whether they were acknowledged to be so or not. We are right in placing Shakespeare and Goethe, for whom the classics were a seed, above Racine, not to mention other more servile imitators, for whom they were a model. But you will agree that the process of development of a seed is more intricate and more difficult to follow than the process of reproduction of a model. It is much easier to show the influence of the classics on Racine than on Shakespeare or Goethe. Yes, of course it is; but the statement of a problem does not cancel the necessity of solving it. The history of literature as a science is still only in its infancy. The well-known writer Taine gave it a great impetus forward when he insisted that literature should be considered a product of the society from which and for which it was created. It is not less important, however, to insist that, apart from these external forces, we should track out that inner force also which lived and lives in it, namely classical literature. "Modern works," to repeat the words of Montesquieu, "were written for the reader, ancient for the writer," and consequently, let us add, for those also who study and criticise these writers.

Let us now glance a little back. In our review of the ancient world we began, as was natural, with religion. Religion brought us to mythology, mythology to literature, literature to philosophy. We have so far considered philosophy as merely a type of literature; let us now proceed to discuss its independent signification as philosophy, properly so called. In this subject more than elsewhere we are struck forcibly by the degree to which the Greek people were, to repeat Vladimir Solovioff's expression, "many-thoughted." At the present day the English and the Germans are the most creative peoples in the sphere of philosophy. The former have been always inclined to empiricism, the latter to rationalism. In regard to the Greeks, however, it is difficult to say which of these two directions of thought lay nearer to their hearts. Greece produced the rationalist Plato, but also the empiricist Democritus. Both streams were united in Aristotle, but then again separated one from the other. The direction in which Plato pointed was followed by the Stoics, Democritus' path by Epicurus. This saving duality in philosophic thought Greece bequeathed to the modern world also. Henceforward a deadening, one-sided philosophy was impossible. By turns now Plato, now Epicurus enriched and revived modern philosophy. The rationalism of Plato blended with religion, the empiricism of Epicurus with science. The first was born an idealist, the second a materialist. The first leads us to the improvement of man as such, the second to man's power over Nature. Both paths are necessary for us, but the most necessary thing of all is the struggle between them, that fruitful rivalry the result of which is man's progress in culture. God forfend that either of these two roads be blocked, that human reason wander either into the barren desert of speculation or into the miry slough of purely material interests. To preclude the chance of such a calamity we should never abandon ancient philosophy; yes, ancient philosophy, I say, with its healthy universalism which scans with a clear gaze heaven and earth alike. . . . But, perhaps, this is too difficult a subject to discuss here. You know that we cannot exhaust our immediate themes; I can show you only small specimen-pictures. Such a one I shall now exhibit from the world of ancient philosophy. From its many aspects I shall choose one for our consideration, namely moral philosophy.

That is a question which affects all of us alike. Morality is essential to every society. The morality of our day is Christian morality, which is accepted even by those who are more or less unsympathetic towards the religious truths of Christianity. It is remarkable, however, that the first Christian thinkers, on becoming acquainted with ancient philosophy, were struck by its majesty and purity. In their attitude towards it they showed the religious spirit of Christians and the honourable spirit of thinkers. They devised the following explanation of it: "The Lord God," they said, "in his care for the human race before the coming of Christ, gave to the Hebrews law and to the Greeks philosophy." Notice that juxtaposition—to the Hebrews law, to the Greeks philosophy. Law says, "you must," or "you must not," and that is all. Philosophy sets everywhere the questions "why?" and "for what purpose?" Thus we mark a difference in the attitude of the Creator towards the two chosen peoples. The Hebrews he ordered, with the Greeks he reasoned. Such, at any rate to my mind, is the natural logical deduction to be drawn from the attitude taken by the Holy Fathers. I shall not pursue the idea, however, lest I stumble into heresy. I shall confine myself to the Greeks.

Even with them morality did not bear a philosophical stamp from the very beginning. They also had laws and commandments, the author of which was considered to be Chiron, the first teacher of morality, the tutor of Achilles and other heroes. The first commandment was: "Pay honour to Zeus and the other gods"; the second: "Honour your parents"; and the third: "Do not ill-treat your guest and stranger." These were the three great commandments of Chiron, Χειρῶνος ὑποθῆκαι, the breaking of which was a deadly sin punished by eternal penalties in the other world. But, of course, this was not all. There was a whole system of moral philosophy which sheltered itself with the supreme sanction of a revelation—"these ether-born laws," as Sophocles calls them, "the father of which was Olympus alone. It was not human nature that produced them, and so they will not be buried under the tomb of forgetfulness." Pindar, Æschylus, Herodotus, Sophocles—there you have the main sources of these laws, of the ancient morality enjoined by laws. In what light are we to consider them? We are not bound to believe in Chiron and Olympus. We may contradict the great Greek poet and say that it was just human nature that produced these commandments, that law of selection which is as strong in the moral world as in the physical. That cycle of moral rules which guarantee to a community the most favourable conditions for its development is created by the law of selection; it is a result at which mankind has arrived unconsciously after many ages of experience.

Of course, if we consider the instinctive morality of the ancient Greeks from this point of view only, it does not stand higher than the instinctive morality of any other civilised or barbarous people. All alike are defined by one and the same irresistible law of selection. What, then, is the reason for the exceptional importance of Greek morality? It is the fact that Greek civilisation, crossing over to Rome and transmitted by Rome to modern nations, is the only civilisation in the history of mankind which has conquered and is conquering. All the other civilisations, not excluding even those most tenacious of life, namely the Mahommedan and the Buddhist, are civilisations that have been conquered or are in process of being conquered. Here we stand on quite firm biological ground. The instinctive morality of the Greek people is the most healthy of all—and the most healthy because it has created the one permanent civilisation in the world. But does that imply that it should be a model for us? Of course not. We have seen already that models generally should not be sought for in the ancient world. But if any instinctive morality deserves the attention of our age, it is the Greek beyond all question; and that attention has been, and is being paid to it in full measure, ever since the time when Fr. Nietzsche rose up among us as its missionary. . . .

It was not this instinctive morality, however, about which I wished to speak at this point, but about that conscious philosophical morality which rose up in its stead, after one of the greatest reforms through which humanity has lived in the sphere of morals. That reform is bound up with the name of Socrates. And the means whereby Socrates brought about such a revolution in Athens was nothing else than the setting of the question "why?" and "for what purpose?" in regard to every single moral principle or law. In this relation Socrates himself, and the moral philosophy that originated with him, occupy a perfectly peculiar position. The history of mankind does not know another similar example. If the pre-Socratic instinctive morality awakens our interest as the most precious of all instinctive systems of morality, so the Socratic conscious system deserves our attention as being unique. And Socrates, as you know, paid dearly for his initiative. His contemporaries were horrified at these "whys?" and "for what purposes?" of his, to which they did not know an answer, and to which he himself knew no answer. You remember his melancholy words: "They all know nothing, and I, too, am not wiser than they. I know only that I know nothing, whereas they do not know even this." Instinctive morality had ceased to satisfy thinking minds, and the new conscious morality was not yet in existence. The Athenian community felt itself in the position of people who have pushed off from one bank and do not see the other. Socrates deprived his fellow-citizens of that spiritual food which had been hitherto their nourishment. Let us not err in harshness while considering their protest against him. On the other hand, let us not withhold our admiration from that bold swimmer who has plunged off resolutely from the shore in search of a new better world. The questions set by Socrates were answered by later thinkers, especially the Stoics. The result of their answers was a moral philosophy from which originated the only so-called autonomous ethical system in the world, a system which deduces a man's moral duty from his nature, once properly understood.

But, I may be asked, what need have we of that ethical system when we have the morality of Christianity? In the first place, I have protested once before against this separation of Christianity from the ancient world. There are no reasons for this distinction save the purely external one, that classical thought has always been and is studied in the Philosophical Faculty and Christianity in the Theological Faculty. How is it possible to distinguish from Antiquity that force for civilisation which originated and developed within the boundaries of the Roman empire in the epoch of the first Roman emperors and appeared as an answer to the eternal questions of ancient thought? And, indeed, every student of the history of Christianity and Christian ethics knows that the last was nourished on the sap of that ancient philosophy which, in the words of the Christian Fathers themselves, was given by God to the Hellenes before the coming of Christ. But that argument is not the one to which I attach importance. You can overturn it by pointing to the fact that Christian morality is, in its principle, distinct from pre-Socratic and from Socratic morality. There we had instinctive morality and conscious morality, whereas here we have revealed morality. I shall not dispute the point ; I would only raise a question. Is it desirable that the only sanction of moral duty should be a revelation ? Many, I know, will be inclined to answer : "Yes." Again I shall not argue the point as to principle. I shall join issue only as to facts.

Religious scepticism is a fact, and a fact, too, not nearly so terrible as many people represent it. Within certain limits it may even be regarded as a biological phenomenon. There is a period in a man's life—and it is just the age, gentlemen, at which you now are—when it is as if wings were growing on his soul. That is due partly to the mighty inrush of life forces in a healthy organism, partly to the fact that an ever wider and wider horizon is opening before the eyes of youth. The young man looks with a conqueror's gaze at that space which has opened before him. He feels himself master of it, if not at present, at any rate in the future. To all reminders of a troublesome higher sanction he is disposed to answer : "I believe in myself and in my own strength." Later on, when the spring floods subside into their normal channels, he becomes sobered, weighs his strength with his problem, learns to respect that sanction which he formerly repudiated. This change has nothing in common with that metamorphosis which I indicated before. It is honourable and disinterested, and I am actually sorry for the man who "in his youth was not young." I recall Petrarch's words: "The tree which has not bloomed in spring does not bear fruit in autumn." ("Non fructificat autumno arbor quæ vere non floruit.") Sometimes even whole communities live through such periods of intensified life and daring thought. One of the periods—the age of Locke and Voltaire—discovered the meaning of the autonomous morality of Socrates' school. We ourselves, too, have seen the pre-Socratic instinctive morality communicated to the consciousness of the modern world by just such another outburst of youthful enthusiasm. Its regenerator chose as index and symbol the ancient god of the spring and returning vigour, Dionysus. Such phenomena are far from having a merely temporary significance. Of course, every exaggeration passes. The force of Voltaire has passed, that of Nietzsche will pass also. Only the struggle will not pass, that unique and indispensable means of effecting improvement.

Such a struggle lies before us also, perhaps the most serious of all that have ever agitated humanity. And in these periods, when the violence of the contest is enhanced, we should not confine ourselves within the limits of any one moral code, even though it be Christian. New social combinations are maturing, and with them also new problems of individual and public ethics. For their solution we cannot be satisfied with those rules which we have received handed down from our fathers and forefathers. We must verify their right to existence, we must penetrate through that alluvial stratum of current morality to the real morality which is supported on the firm foundation of human nature, and not merely human nature—that was the mistake of the enlightened period—but our European nature, the roots of which are fixed in our spiritual mother country—namely Antiquity. And that is why we must turn from our morals both to the pre-Christian, the Socratic, and to the pre-Socratic, the instinctive, not to re-establish them, God forfend, but that the new system of which we stand in need may be produced from their struggle with current morality.

Such is the need of the time. Many signs make it clear that we are going to see a revival of interest in the classical world which will not only be better understood, but also exercise a profounder influence on society. Friedrich Nietzsche is only one example, one symptom. The extraordinary, though indeed deferred success of that prophet of Antiquity—and that, too, the most ancient pre-Socratic Antiquity—clearly shows us in what direction contemporary problems point and where the means of solving them is to be found. With us in Russia people have always been especially sensitive to moral questions and problems. In Russia the public consciousness has been less hampered by traditional frames than in other countries, and strains more boldly out towards space, from the conditional and transitory to the real, the natural, the eternal. Consequently interest in the classical peoples should be stronger in Russia than anywhere. And when I hear in our midst that crusade of hate and contempt toward Antiquity, I fancy that I am in presence of some colossal and shameful misunderstanding. I would like to cry out to society: "Why! what are you doing? You've got before you a bowl of the most sparkling, the most tasty, the most nourishing beverage, but because its edge is smeared with wormwood, you turn peevishly away like a child!"

Enough, however, as to ancient philosophy. Its characteristics have by themselves led us to the social and political formations of the ancient world, to the practice and the theory of ancient polity. Yes, the practice and the theory; by placing these two terms in juxtaposition we mark clearly the distinguishing feature of ancient politics. One form or another of social and political life has been essential to all the peoples of the ancient and modern worlds, but only the classical nations have thought, judged, and written about it, and those moderns who learnt from Antiquity to do so.

One sphere, indeed, of that life among all civilised peoples has called for a conscious attitude towards it—namely the sphere of justice. To regulate the relations between citizens and also between half-citizens, and to check to some degree at least the arbitrary license of brute force, a definite legislation was needed, made up of a series of definite prescriptions: "If any one does so and so, he is subjected to so and so." The most ancient of these codes, that of Hammurabi of Babylon, which relates to a period three thousand years before Christ, was found not so long ago, and the discovery aroused universal interest among civilised nations. That code is, indeed, extremely interesting, among other reasons because we learn from it how long humanity lived on what may be called mere trade prescriptions of the pattern: "If any one does so and so, he is subjected to so and so," and how great must have been the exploit of that people which alone could rise above these prescriptions to a scientific jurisprudence, that had as its basis precise and definite legal terms, and in its code an illustration of how to work with them. That achievement is as great an exploit of thought as progress from wise women's practices to scientific medicine, which has as its basis a knowledge of the qualities of organisms and substances. That change in the world of justice was realised partly by the Greeks but especially by the Romans, and that fact is the reason why Roman law has been, is, and will be the source of nourishment for modern jurisprudence.

I know that this position is frequently combated, not so much, however, by jurists *qua* jurists—I make this juridical reservation inasmuch as jurists themselves are often members of a party, and as members of a party say, of course, what their party bids them—as by non-jurists and quasi-jurists. "Why should we learn Roman law ? " they ask. " Our conceptions of marriage, of the family, and so on—how are they Roman ? How can the model of Roman law help us ? " Notice—the model. Everywhere one and the same delusion. The model is inapplicable, so, forsooth, there is nothing to learn. We ridicule the soldier in the well-known story who refused to solve the arithmetical problem : " If I gave you five roubles and you sent three to your wife, how many would be left ? " on the ground that nobody had given him five roubles, and that he was a bachelor. As a matter of fact, however, these quasi-jurists, whose opinions I have just quoted, are not a whit wiser than the soldier. It is not the model of Roman law that we need. We need the legal conceptions which that chosen people of Themis created of such astonishingly precise and serviceable character—all those *justum* and *aequum*, *dolus* and *culpa*, *possessio* and *dominium*, *hereditas* and *legatum*, *fideicommissum*, *usufructus*, *servitus obligatio*, and countless others. We need the ability to use these terms, recognise their application in given legal relations, and therewith lead the complicated individual cases of actual life to comparatively simple formulæ. We need all that fine and acute juridical analysis of which the Roman lawyers were masters. " But why ? " the quasi-jurists ask ; " these terms and their usage, as far as they are necessary, have been taken over into modern law." And in modern law, I ask, have they ceased to be Roman ? You have replaced the word *usufructus* by the corresponding term in

Russian—do you imagine that, thanks to that simple manipulation, you have obtained a Russian code instead of the Roman ? You have torn off the label from an amphora of choice Falernian wine and glued on a Russian ticket—do you console yourself with the thought that you are drinking a home-produced vintage ? That short-sighted partisanship of modern times is pernicious for but this reason, that it leads to such shameless falsifications and plagiarisms.

But that is only one aspect of the subject. I put aside à priori the "model" character forced upon Antiquity, and disregarded the corresponding principle in my appraisement. None the less, here and there we might find some instruction in this relation also, and in the field of Roman law far more than elsewhere. Even that, however, is not all. Whatever attitude one adopts toward the immediate actual significance of Roman law, the value which it *had* for us as the origin of our law and the source of nourishment for our jurisdiction cannot be taken from it; "habere eripi potest, habuisse non potest," in Seneca's admirable phrase. We cannot learn the history of our law without learning Roman law, and we cannot avoid learning that history if we would stand in at all conscious relations to that which is a vital and essential part of our world. The answer to a question about the sense of legal institutions brings us to their origin: the answer to a question about their origin leads to their history, that is, as I have said, to Roman law. Whoever is ignorant of it will never be a jurist-thinker; and such men were never so urgently needed as to-day, when there is going on a decomposition, so to say, of the capital code and process, and when the brooding conscience of humanity, in the persons of Tolstoy, Nietzsche, and Hæckel, is raising ever fresh questions for jurisprudence to solve and waiting with intense anxiety for the answers.

But law and jurisprudence form only one aspect of what may be termed ancient "politics" in the classical sense of that word. There are many other aspects, so many that we cannot think of even a roughly filled in sketch. In the foundation of all the other states of Antiquity lies either a military or a financial idea. Greece alone revealed the thought that a state forms a means toward moral education and progress. This idea is not met with so early as in Homer. The Homeric community, in spite of many attractive features, acts on us like Nature itself with its rough material simplicity. But then Delphi, the greatest, wisest, and most moral force in Greece right down to the fifth century, takes on itself the stupendous problem of giving Greece a political education in the spirit of the Apollonic religion and morality. The Greek people had ere now divided into small independent communities, each with a population of some thousands. These πόλεις were material suitable in the highest degree for the important and instructive experiments about to be performed on them. One must search far and wide in modern history to find anything parallel. As an example, one might cite Geneva in the time of Calvin. The experiments were carried out with various means and various degrees of success. In some communities, Sparta, for example, Delphi succeeded in taking the government into its own hands. In others, as in Athens, it met with co-operation from strong parties in the state. In others, again, as in the south Italian colonies, the instrument it used was the powerful Orphic order. Here Delphi conquered, there its efforts were idle. All these spectacles are equally interesting to us. An experiment of a different nature and in opposition to Delphi was tried by the Athenian politicians of the fifth century. But the landless community of warriors and officials which it created was overturned in the Peloponnesian war. The theory of the fourth century—the ideas of Plato in his "Republic"—benefited by the practical experiments, but again only to pass the sooner into practice.

So Greece bequeathed to us, both in theoretical exposition and in practical application, principles of politics in the broadest sense of the word. The question which it set itself, namely, what is the way to build a state so as to secure for individuals the possibility of the greatest moral progress? runs like a red thread through all these experiments and constructions. It is a question of the most absorbing interest. The very fact that the Greeks put it in this form showed an immense step forward. "What is the way to build a state so that . . ." that is to say, a state is not something elemental. It depends on ourselves to build and rebuild it according to the aim which we consider best. So the ancients believed, so they have taught us to believe. This idea was at one time the source of extravagant exaggerations and delusions. In the age of enlightenment thinkers exaggerated the power of reason to govern the will, and imagined that they needed only well-conceived constitutions to educate the masses from their darkness and create a new race of people. The bloody history of the French Revolution, with its still-born constitution and savage outbursts of fury, has taught us to look more soberly at the facts and not despise that blind elemental factor which is inherent in the character of any given community. But the essence of the idea of political progress which Antiquity has bequeathed to us was not itself touched thereby. That was one step in advance. The second was the conception of the moral signification of a state in its relation toward individuals. This conception contained the roots of the struggle between ideas equally precious and equally important for the progress of civilisation, the idea of citizenship and the idea of individual freedom. Delphi insisted on the first and subordinated individuality to the state. Athens tried to emancipate individuality, as far as that was possible without detriment to the power of the state. This tendency of the Athenian empire is clearly emphasised by Pericles in his funeral speech in Thucydides' history. So Antiquity introduced into the world that fruitful political antithesis, the antagonism between socialistic and individualistic principles, and the more conscious champions in modern history of the one or the other cause have always acknowledged themselves to be the pupils of Antiquity and have highly prized its signification. The father of contemporary socialism, Ferdinand Lassalle, saw in classical education a happy counterpoise to the bourgeois philosophy of the Germany of his time. He counted it "the firm bedrock of the German spirit." It was from Antiquity that his antipodes, Nietzsche, the prophet of extreme individualism, borrowed those principles on which he insisted in his preaching with such eloquence and success. Both were right, inasmuch as both were so far educated that they counted Antiquity not a model for, but a seed of modern civilisation.

But in this matter also we must admit not only the vast theoretical significance of ancient polity but its great historical importance as well. The term "historical" I ask you to understand not in the sense of its being foreign to the modern world but in the sense of its being exceedingly near to it. I said once before that our past is not a past in the proper meaning of the word. It lives in us and we live by it. In studying the past we study our present conditions in all their most stable and lasting features. Try to look at the present as if you had been born to-day, as if you knew nothing even about yesterday. Everything you see appears equally valuable, indispensable, and eternal. The institution of high neck-ties or ladies' flat-shaped hats seems on a line with the institution of the hard or soft final sign or the letter "yaht," with the institution of military conscription or jurymen's courts, with the institution of marriage and friendship. What will help you to distinguish the temporary from the eternal, mere caprice from necessity, the essential from the unessential? An accurate knowledge of mankind? But that is a science of the future, indeed of the distant future. For the time being our only guide is the past. And if we classical students are transported by our thoughts into the distant past of our civilisation, it is not with the object of flying away from our age but of understanding it more easily and thoroughly, of passing from the conditional and transitional to the unconditional and eternal, or at any rate the lasting, of being able to appreciate correctly the phenomena all round us and distinguish the alluvial layer which to-morrow's wave will wash away from the granite bedrock on which our civilisation rests. Its history begins for us where the history of Greece begins. I need not speak of the history of the East. It is unknown how far the history of Greece may be considered its continuation. When we study that beginning and compare it with modern life, we learn to recognise the path on which humanity strides forward, led by its stern educator, the law of sociological selection.

And, as I observed before, a study of that path gives us not only mental knowledge but spiritual boldness and courage as well, inspired by the comforting agreement of biological and moral values. Only at this point, indeed, throughout the long path of the life of society do these two values coincide—for the short space of individual life they now approach and now depart from each other, baffling us with their combinations. I recall the half-jesting, half-serious lines of a Russian epigrammatist :

> Whoe'er at forty is no pessimist,
> Or at fifty no misanthropist,
> Perhaps is pure in heart,
> But he'll fill an idiot's grave.

Yes, an idiot like Karatayeff, Akim, or the character that Dostoyevski has described. . . . It is indeed true that throughout the life of one generation might triumphs over right at every step, and littleness over both ; and even that is not the worst. Of course, it is sad to see so many fair lives spoiled in the triumph of self-satisfied worthlessness and baseness. It is still sadder, however, to see the wreck of noble ideas, to see the corpses of butchered truth in newspaper columns and other organs of public opinion. What can we do ? Throughout mere human life you grow acquainted only with the small " I " of the society in which you live—and it is not very comforting. If you wish to know its great " I "—that force which directs the law of sociological selection—you must go back to the past and study the path of human civilisation from the earliest beginnings. And here you will notice what I referred to just now—the coincidence of biological and moral values. Its essence may be expressed as follows: "Bad proves unsuited for life and becomes extinct, good suited for life and survives or is revived." You are filled with a bright hope of that mysterious future whither the inscrutable Will is carrying us; you approve of Nicolas Lenau's * fine words in their application to human nature:

> Love nature; she is just and true,
> She strives for freedom and for happiness.

* The real name of this Austrian poet (1802–50) was Niembsch. He borrowed the name Lenau from his estate Strehlenau. His principal works are a Faust, Savonarola, Albigeois, and one or two volumes of shorter poems.

For the characters alluded to on p. 167 and Count Aleksai Tolstoy, the epigrammatist, see Appendix.

LECTURE VII

BOTH my preceding lectures were devoted to the signification of classical study as a force for culture. I dealt with a fairly wide diversity of subjects—religion, mythology, literature, philosophy, law, politics. These subjects, however, were connected by common attachment to the sphere of Antiquity, and also by being looked at from a common standpoint. I tried throughout to prove to you that Antiquity ought to be for us not a model, but a seed. This reservation is of the highest importance. It lifts us at once above all parties, not merely political, but of any nature whatever. I will illustrate by an example what that means. You may have noticed that I have carefully avoided in my lectures the word "classicism." I did so not because that word grates on the ears of many members of our society—in that connection, I hope, no one will reproach me with cowardice—but because the very idea which it denotes does not correspond with what I consider useful and profitable for our present purpose. By classicism we mean an attitude towards literature and art which sees in the literature and art of Antiquity — and not of all Antiquity, but only of a conspicuous part of it—precisely a model for imitation. In that sense classicism is opposed on the one hand to romanticism, on the other to naturalism. The attitude is one which has equal rights with both of those just cited, but only equal rights—nothing more. In Antiquity, however, we seek what may suit alike classicists, romanticists, and followers of the " natural " school. We seek, as I have said many times before, not models, but seeds.

This consideration should be borne in view in the next aspect of Antiquity to which we are now turning, to finish with it our survey of the whole field. This is the sphere of art. Art in our case means especially architecture, sculpture, and painting, but the term extends also to domestic and other furniture, as far as such objects bear an artistic character.

Let us begin with architecture.

Its fundamental characteristics in Antiquity are very simple—the Greek column with the straight entablature, and the arch which may be considered pre-eminently Roman. It is worth our while, however, to reflect on the structural idea which is embodied in these principles. Two pillars and a cross-beam—such is the original scheme of Greek architecture. Gravity presses entirely from above downwards ; it is resisted by the column, the forces of which are directed accordingly entirely from below upwards. It is interesting to see how the whole column is a kind of animated representation of that force which acts from below upwards.

But at present we are interested by one consideration only, namely the profound honesty, if I may use the word, of Greek architecture. The outer appearance of a building fully expresses its structural idea. You can build a Greek temple without any artificial means for lending strength, without cement or iron supports, and it will hold firm. There was only one difficulty to face. With an interval at all considerable between the columns it was difficult to find stone cross-beams of sufficient length. The arch was invented to overcome that obstacle, its principle being a cuneiform section of stones. In this way the ancients became able to surmount the difficulty of quite considerable intervals between columns by stones or bricks of inconsiderable size. This second feature of ancient architecture was also honest, and consequently the vault also along with the dome. You can build an arch of wedge-shaped bricks without cement or artificial claspings, and the arch will not only keep firm itself, but support the upper part of the edifice. The more the weight presses upon it, the more compact and firm the arch itself will be.

But if it removed one difficulty, the arch introduced another, for which Roman architecture did not find a fully satisfactory solution. With the system of the straight entablature the weight pressed, as we have seen, only from above downwards in a vertical direction. With the system of the arch it pressed also from the centre toward both sides in a horizontal direction. Try to build an arch of wedge-shaped bricks over two columns ; it will begin to thrust the columns outwards till they topple over. So a new architectural element was wanted to resist this horizontal pressure also. Roman architecture did not find it and circumvented rather than solved the difficulty. But the direct continuation of Roman architecture was the Romanesque architecture of the early Middle Ages, and its direct continuation again was the Gothic style of the late Middle Ages. This last succeeded in finding a fully satisfactory architectural answer to the question raised by the Roman arch. Since the weight pressed in two directions, vertically and horizontally, but especially in the first, its pictorial representation was an oblique line, the diagonal of the parallelogram of these forces. To overcome it, therefore, one required an element to meet it in a like fashion, that is to say, not directly from below upwards, but in a slanting direction—in other words, a counterpoise. This principle, after some incomplete efforts of Romanesque architecture in the same direction, was adopted into the system of Gothic architecture as an integral and indispensable part. Gothic architecture developed and embellished it, creating both the counter-pillar and the counter-arch. This discovery restored that architectural honesty which had been slightly violated by the introduction of the Roman arch, that architectural honesty which demands that the outer appearance of a building should be the exact expression of the structural idea that informs it.

The history of architecture knows only two examples of that absolute honesty, the Greek style and the Gothic style. We may be told that these two styles are in direct opposition to each other. Yes, of course they are. Their mutual relations are those of vertical to horizontal. As a model Greek style was certainly not used by Gothic style, but no less certainly the latter was only a flower from the seed of Antiquity. That seed was architectural honesty. What that implies we shall see immediately.

The structural principle alone does not make up an architectural style. The decorative principle always shares in it to a greater or less degree. You see this last in the Greek style also. If you ask yourselves what is its relation in Greek architecture to the structural principle, you will see that it was an illustration of the proverb: "To work time, to amusement an hour." Work is here the support of the weight, and the column especially is concerned with that work which is its entire care. The whole appearance of its severely harmonious stem expresses that idea; for amusement, that is to say for ornament, it has no time. Then we come to the architrave. Here the weight and the support, the force that presses from above, and the force that resists the pressure, are, as it were, neutralised. The architrave affords, so to say, a moment of rest. You will notice that here the amusement, that is to say the ornamentation, enters upon its rights; the Ionic scrolls and the Corinthian leaves wind round the capital of the column. But the architrave also has work of its own. It has to support the weight of all the upper part of the entablature which presses on it—in the Doric style—with its triglyphs. On the other hand, the rectangular intervals between the triglyphs are free from work, and note how here again in the so-called metopes the artist's fancy receives full play and the metopes are adorned with sculptural representations. The entablature supports the roof, which in front appears a plane isosceles triangle, the so-called pediment. The space within this triangle again represents a neutral field of repose, and here again, accordingly, you meet sculptural decorations. In this way the same architectural honesty which characterises the structural side of the Greek style is repeated also in its ornamental aspect. The rôle of the second is purely secondary, it never overshadows the structural idea.

The strongest negation, on the other hand, of this principle of architectural honesty is seen first of all in the Eastern styles, and also in the degenerate classical style, influenced partly by Oriental methods. These styles have all one element in common, a fantastic element. What is their speciality? The subordination of the structural principle to the decorative, the perversion of the structural elements to mere ornamental patterns, the concealment of the structural idea behind architectural forms which are themselves impossible? Take the Byzantine style, which is of special importance for Russians. In Stjigovski's happy expression, it represents "Greece in the arms of the East." Notice its bent, pointed arch. Built of wedge-shaped bricks, such an arch would be unable not only to support anything, but even remain firm itself. Its outer appearance does not correspond with a structural idea. It is possible only thanks to plaster cement and artificial supports. Consider the Byzantine column. That main feature of Greek architecture is in this stage given up to utter uselessness. It appears somewhere from some angle and disappears into another without supporting anything, which, however, it could not have supported in any case. In other words, it has been perverted into mere ornamentation. Take Arabian architecture, the Alhambra with its stalactite vaults, which are as impossible structurally as the Byzantine arch. Once again the ornamentor's fancy, with the help of plaster and such things, has concealed the structural element that lies at the bottom of its creation, namely the Roman arch. Take the Russian style and its characteristic peculiarity, the bulbous dome. It is a structural absurdity, possible only owing to the artificial supports hidden within the dome. The effect is that, whereas the props which support it are hidden carefully from us, we are shown that it cannot be supported by itself only. You will agree that this principle is in direct opposition to the principle of architectural honesty of which I have been speaking, and which requires that the outer appearance of a building should correspond with its structural idea. The Russian style is in fashion with us at the present moment, but only because it is Russian. I cannot believe that its success is to be lasting. Such enthusiasm for anti-structural forms has usually been followed in the history of architecture by the revival of classical influence with its sobriety and honesty. I believe that the same thing will happen with us also, but not, of course, with the result of reviving among us the models of Greek or Roman architecture in place of our present ones. No; if the artist-architects of coming generations borrow from ancient architecture its seed, namely architectural honesty, and combine it with the forms of Russian ornamentation, then Russia will have that national style which we both look for and ask for. About the details, of course, it is still premature to hazard conjectures.

So far we have dealt exclusively with ancient architecture. Let us now cast a rapid glance over the other arts also, especially sculpture and painting. In contradistinction to architecture these two arts are imitative. Apart from the conditions of mere technique the artist's style is defined by the questions: whom or what to imitate? in what manner to imitate? The special character of ancient, that is to say again Greek, imitative art, forms an answer to these questions. To understand it let us, on this subject also, start from as elementary a scheme as possible, as simplified as it can conceivably be.

Let us imagine, to begin with, the primitive artist who first, with no predecessor, takes it on himself to portray some object or other—let us say a man. It is, of course, obvious that the representation obtained under these circumstances will be of a purely fortuitous character, according to the way in which the artist regards his object and the way in which his hand obeys his eyes. Then let us imagine that after our first artist another sets himself precisely the same problem. That second artist can stand towards the first in one of three relations. In the first place he can ignore him. In that case, of course, his representation will be just as fortuitous as his predecessor's was. If we imagine subsequently also such an attitude of successor to predecessor we get a fortuitous art without any definite style. In the second place, he may subordinate himself entirely to his predecessor's influence and try to reproduce all the other's manner. If the former represented the human torso as a trapezium resting on a rectangle, then he also will have recourse to the same figure. This relation gives us a conventional art with a very severely defined style, but progressive only in the sense of ever greater and greater emphasising of the conventional elements. Lastly, in the third place, the second artist may divide his attention between his predecessor and the object represented. He studies his predecessor carefully so as to make himself entirely master of his technique, but he is also deeply interested in the object he wishes to portray. He tries to account to himself for those deficiencies which were inherent in his predecessor's manner, and he tries also to come nearer to nature than the latter succeeded in doing. With such a relation you get an art which, like the second, possesses a style—as far as each artist is dependent on his predecessors in regard to technique, but which is also progressive in the sense of showing an ever-increasing freedom from conventionality and approximation to Nature. So there are three possible schemes. Now you know that schemes in their abstract mathematical nicety are never to be met with in reality. With that reservation, we may say that the first, fortuitous art is characteristic of barbarous peoples, the second, conventional art, of the peoples of the near and far East, and that, finally, the third, natural art, was invented by and characteristic of the Greeks alone among ancient nations and practised in modern times by ourselves, the peoples of European civilisation, under the influence of Greek art. Freedom and naturalness—that is the first characteristic feature of ancient art.

It is easy to be convinced that it is so. For this purpose our St. Petersburg Hermitage offers peculiarly rich facilities of which, unfortunately, very little advantage has hitherto been taken. I refer to those memorials of ancient Greek painting which are known by the name of "painted vases," and which occupy several large rooms in the lower storey. There you may observe a collection not of more or less fortuitous character, such as there is in the sculpture gallery, but one that represents a full and complete circle of evolution. The most ancient paintings of the human figure on the brown archaic vases stand but little above a child's wonderful trapezium on a rectangle. Then follow the so-called black-figured vases, with far more natural though still very angular and conventional representations. Further on you meet with red-figured vases, also of different styles—severe, beautiful, free—and you see one conventionality being dropped after another, and the claims of naturalness being satisfied in an ever greater and greater degree. Later still the tension slackens, luxuriousness and carelessness begin to reign, decline and degeneration are at hand. Scarcely anywhere can one follow that deeply instructive evolution with such facility as in the vase department of our Hermitage, and it is painful to see how these beautiful rooms are nearly always empty, and how their treasures remain but buried capital. The Hermitage authorities might do much to mend matters. It depends upon them to come to the assistance of the intelligently interested public and supply, instead of the dry, unintelligible catalogue on sale at present, another that would give more prominence to the evolutionary and artistic signification of our magnificent collection.

Freedom and naturalness—that combination of qualities forms one of the characteristic marks of ancient art. I may observe, too, in this connection that it is thanks chiefly to this feature that ancient art has become the educator of modern art. Its revival always had the effect of teaching artists once more to see and recognise nature and to emancipate them from the conventionality of their epochs ; and in this sphere Antiquity in the best periods of modern art was not a model, but a seed. But that does not exhaust all that there is to be said. In addition to freedom and naturalness, ancient art had still another feature, which was also important. That feature we call idealism. This word, however, requires explanation. It is far less intelligible than it seems at first sight. As applied to ancient art, the term does not refer to the fact that the Greeks represented principally gods and goddesses, and not ordinary mortals, and beauty preferably to monstrosity or vulgarity —that was in consequence of external conditions which made the statues of Apollo or Heracles more in demand on the market than figures of fishermen or drunk women. No, idealism passes throughout the whole sphere of ancient art, not excluding even those two last subjects. We shall even find it easier to understand and estimate this quality by considering the latter rather than the former class of persons.

Let us take an artist set the task of representing a fisherman. As I said before, he is a realist, so he will seek the fisherman first of all in nature. But nature does not give him a fisherman simply or even a Greek fisherman simply. It gives him a fisherman Phrynichus or Komius, that is to say, a figure whose outlines characterise it as not only a fisherman, but also Phrynichus or Komius. Now these last features are interesting only for the fisherman's personal acquaintances, whereas the first interest all those who are interested in general in the fisherman type. And now the artist asks himself: what is there in that aggregation of marks which I see before me that characterises their possessor as being just a fisherman? What, in other words, expresses the idea of fisherman? Corresponding with his solution of that question he makes his figure. His aim is to collect, if possible, all the marks that are characteristic of a fisherman as such and remove, if possible, all the fortuitous features characteristic of the individual on whom he happened to light. Of course, the ability to note these marks was not given to the Greeks all at once. There was a time when their only way of representing a fisherman was to represent a man, or at best a vulgar man, and aim at intelligibility by putting a rod or caught fish in his hands. All their skill was won in process of time. And that ability of theirs to distinguish the marks of the species from the marks of the race on the one hand, and those of the individual on the other, beyond doubt expresses the character of that intellectual people who created logic and philosophy generally.

Such is the idealism of ancient art. Its essence, as you see, is the demand that a representation should answer to the idea of the object represented. Of course, the highest creations of that idealism are to be seen in the superhuman sphere, in the sphere of gods and heroes. There the Greeks hold not merely the first, but the only place, unrivalled by any other people. Many peoples had felt the need of representing their gods and understood also that for the artist divinity means superhumanity, but whereas all other nations understood that term in the sense of monstrosity, the Greeks alone conceived it in the meaning of beauty. Superhuman beauty was a creation of the ancient genius which has taught us also to understand and reproduce it. That one point, however, does not exhaust the educative rôle of ancient art in the field surveyed by us here—that is only one of the aspects of ancient idealism. But all its aspects have been necessary to us at various periods of the development of our art and will be necessary while our art will be developed in future, that is to say, let us hope, necessary always. And that idealism is easily connected with the first characteristic of ancient art which I noticed, its desire for naturalness and freedom. In reality, the greatest idealist in our accepted sense of the word is Nature herself, in her efforts toward the separation and individualisation of species. The ancient artist only anticipates or continues the work of Nature; he creates by the same law of selection which is incumbent upon her also. . . .

But this is, perhaps, too intricate and difficult a thought to be pursued here with the short time at our disposal. Before parting, however, with art, and therewith also with the signification of Antiquity generally for modern culture, I should like to draw attention to one feature of the so-called "artistic industry" of Antiquity—a subject of special importance and interest for our age, in view of similar attempts in the modern development of that sphere of human activity.

That is its "animated" character. For the ancient his objects of use and instruments of work were not simply what they nominally were, but the incarnations or personifications of the forces acting in them or the functions fulfilled by them. When I spoke about the column I mentioned that it appeared to the ancient as the incarnation of the force that acted from below upwards and supported the building. The expression of that force was the slight but very noticeable "swelling" or tension —ἔντασις—of the column, in consequence of which its profile represented not a straight, but a slightly swelling line. We can trace the same influence at work everywhere. Take the ancient pitcher—hydria. When it is set down it seems to grow up from the earth. It is filled with forces that come out of the earth, and so it has the form of a soap bubble blown up from below; it is thicker at the top than at the bottom. A weight, on the other hand, hangs down. The force in it acts from above downwards, and so its form is that of a skin full of water or sand and hanging down; it is thicker at the bottom than at the top. Take a poker: its business, so to say, is to pick among the embers of the fire-pan, and so its end is made in the shape of a man's finger. The legs of a table, again, are made like animals' feet, with claws sticking firmly into the floor. Take the battering-ram, used to break down walls at a siege. Its action produced an impression of butting, and so its extremity was fashioned like a ram's head. All these instances are, of course, trifles, but these trifles express a great metaphysical idea—the idea of a world Will, the development of which was the task set before the philosophy of the latest times.

And now my rapid survey of the significance of Antiquity for modern culture is finished. I have not said, of course, even the tenth part of what might have been said on this theme, but, as you are aware, a full exposition did not indeed enter into my purpose. I wished to bring before you merely small pictures. If you have mastered the fundamental idea of my outline—namely that Antiquity should be for us not a model, but a seed, then you will easily understand also the most important deduction to be drawn from it. That is that the significance of Antiquity for our culture will never cease, and that our link with it will be closer and more intimate with every century. Our culture has come from that seed. It cannot boast of a single at all essential idea which could not be proved with absolutely convincing arguments to have developed organically from it. We have enriched many times, and we will enrich hereafter with it, the seed-plots of our culture, saving them from exhaustion and degeneration—just as we come to the help of our declining vines and other plants by introducing such seeds or shoots from the original nursery or vineyard.

And how strange it is! While every introduction of the seed of Antiquity has raised the level of our culture and created immortal works to serve in their turn as patterns for posterity, the introduction of seeds foreign to our culture has given rise only to hybrids incapable of further multiplication. In the time of Goethe there was Arabomania, to which he himself yielded in his "Eastern-Western Divan." Then followed Indomania, the bloom of which was the philosophy of Schopenhauer—not all of it, fortunately, but only the most sterile part, the pessimism that is linked unorganically with the healthy, fruitful Platonism. Nowadays Japanomania has become the fashion. It has given us many monstrosities of so-called decadent art and is doomed to entire disappearance, unless one is to count the harmless and unreal influence it exercises on our decorative arts. All these are remarkable phenomena which encourage the biological attitude toward the history of civilisation and culture; for, as you know, animal stocks also are improved by means of cross-breeding, only not with different species, however perfect they be—such a method produces only hybrids incapable of multiplication—but with pre-eminent individuals of the same species, those in which the characteristic marks have attained the highest possible degree of perfection.

And that is why we should keep the door leading to Antiquity open. It can help us both now and still more in the process of time. For that purpose it is not at all necessary that all the members of any given society shall pass through the furnace of classical education—if any one understood my initial lectures in that sense, he was mistaken. What, then, is wanted? Only that each community should contain a certain percentage of people with a classical education, and among them, again, a comparatively small amount of people who have consecrated their lives to the study of Antiquity and its application to the wants of the day. Such persons will be occupied, so to say, with procuring the seeds. These seeds will be received by the wider circle of people with a classical education in order to exchange their fruits with people educated in the modern sides of schools, or having an applied technical education. That will constitute the exchange of intellectual goods of which I spoke before. As you may infer from what I say, society needs not only classical secondary schools but several types of such schools, according to the complex nature of its own organism and the diversity of human faculties. It is self-obvious that I, as a man having pretensions to culture, cherish no hostility against any one of these types. Hostility I feel, and that, too, an implacable hostility towards only the "universal school," which at one time threatened us, that still-born child of educational adventurers, which would drive all faculties alike under one common yoke.

. . . .

I have now discussed two divisions of our programme—namely the value of Antiquity for education and its importance for modern culture. Now I must proceed to consider the third aspect of our subject and explain to you its signification as a science. In other words, I must show you what is the essence of the science which deals with Antiquity, or as it is customarily called, classical study. For this third part of my discourse I have left, unfortunately, very little time. I console myself with the reflection that those of you whom this subject interests more or less immediately, that is to say, those of you who intend to study classics at the university, will have the opportunity of hearing my course of lectures in the Classical Faculty. As for the rest of the class, if any of you feel interested enough to pursue the matter, I can do no more than indicate my article "Philology," in Brokhaus and Ephron's Encyclopædia. That article, of course, was written with the dryness which is the inevitable concomitant of dictionary articles. As a counterpoise to that unattractive quality I shall permit myself here to give a short rapid survey, my chief purpose being to develop the third of the antitheses with which I started at the outset. It refers to the point which we are now discussing. We formulated it somewhat as follows: "The world has grown accustomed to think of classics as a thoroughly investigated science which has no more interesting problems to offer to creative work. But men aware of the true position of matters will tell you that it is now more interesting than ever, that all the work of preceding generations was merely preparatory, merely the foundation on which we are only now beginning to build the actual fabric of our knowledge, that new problems beckoning us to investigation and solution meet us at every step in this field of science."

The first part of this antithesis does, indeed, accurately represent the opinion of society—and not merely of so-called "society," but also frequently of people who stand in closer relations to the subject. One of my students, an able and energetic man, was pitchforked by Fate into the Oriental Faculty and became passionately attached to the history of the East. With a neophyte's enthusiasm, he wrote that the history of the East is far more interesting than the history of Greece, inasmuch as it has been far less investigated. These words led me to reflections of this nature. The history of the East is far more interesting —why? Because it has been far less investigated. And when it has been investigated, will it cease to be interesting? If so, then the student's duty is to turn interesting into uninteresting studies. It is worth while to meditate over this question. And, indeed, what is science for us? What do we consider to be its value? I do not speak, of course, about so-called applied science, but about pure science, of which classical scholarship forms one branch. Are we to see in science merely a great head-splitting labour like those toys for children and grown-ups, whose puzzle—taking off a ring from a cross and so on—interests you only till you find the solution ? Or is there something else in it absolutely valuable, and do we, its representatives, work not merely for our own satisfaction to banish ennui, but indeed for the good of mankind ?

It is clear that the second alternative is more in harmony with public opinion, otherwise society would certainly not maintain universities, academies, and libraries at its expense and feed a multitude of people whose only vocation is the study of science and the solution of its problems. And if science as such is interesting and valuable, then it is obvious that its interest grows and does not diminish with its investigation. So I am fully justified in telling my friend that he is mistaken. Greek history is far more interesting than Oriental, and just because it has been far more investigated. That rough labour, the results of which are valuable not in themselves, but because they are the hypotheses or weapons for other positively valuable results—that rough labour, I say, in classical study has already been largely done. That formed precisely the work of former generations, and we ought to be grateful to them for their honourable and disinterested services.

And what is that rough labour ? you ask. I answer, first of all, the collection of records. In classical study a record is the first element of scientific work, just as a number in arithmetic, or an individual in natural history, or a phenomenon in physics. The records with which the classical student has to deal are of different kinds. To begin with, the country itself which was the scene of the history of the ancient peoples, and not merely in its external features, but also in its geological, botanical, and meteorological aspects. Oral tradition and customs are also records when they have descended in unbroken continuity from the early generations to the modern inhabitants. Next, the immediate works of the ancients, which have survived up to our day, even though in a mutilated appearance, whether they be ruins of buildings, or statues, or vases, or inscriptions. Finally, the text of this or that writer, preserved for us even in late mediæval manuscripts. We distinguish between these four types—geographical, ethnological, archæological, and philological. It is their collection which made and makes the first necessary condition for fruitful study—but not merely their collection. During these fifteen hundred to two thousand years which separate us from the ancient world they have been exposed to important changes. The outlines of the shores and the courses of the rivers have altered. Popular legends have been mutilated in transition from one generation to another. Statues or vases survive in a merely fragmentary condition. Texts have suffered from the ignorance or misplaced ingenuity of copyists. It was necessary, therefore, to restore them, as far as possible, to their original appearance by subjecting them to what is called classical criticism.

All this formed the rough labour of which I spoke. I have told you already that it formed the main task of preceding generations, to whom we owe our existing admirable collections—historical atlases, the so-called corpora of inscriptions, bas-reliefs, money, and so on. These collections make it possible for us to work comfortably and profitably in our sphere of science, to study and shed light on the most interesting and intimate aspects of the life of the ancient world. None the less, we cannot say that the work of collecting records is finished—there is much to be done still. Excavations in Greece, Italy, and elsewhere—among other places in our own country, in the territory of the Greek colonists in the south of Russia—have never been interrupted and continue to enrich our treasure house with records, especially archæological records. The last ten years have been marked by unexpected, and occasionally quite wonderful, discoveries of Egyptian papyri with classical texts that had been given up for lost. Thus there were found the treatise of Aristotle about the Athenian state, charming genre scenes of Herodas, speeches of Hyperides, a contemporary of Demosthenes, odes and ballads of Bacchylides, a contemporary of Pindar, and quite lately a nome of Timotheus, the only representative we have of that enigmatical type of lyrical poetry. And, of course, that is not all—the sure sands of Egypt contain still many treasures, and each day we may expect news that there has been found some pearl of ancient literature, poems of Sappho, for example, or comedies of Menander. . . . Our fathers did not know that feeling. In their time the gaps in ancient literature were considered as finally and irretrievably void. I repeat: never yet has classical study been so interesting as now.

But, of course, its interest does not lie merely in the fact that the material for study is constantly being enlarged by fresh discoveries. The chief point is that, thanks to the work of former generations, we can address ourselves to our science with vastly more important questions than our predecessors could. Thanks to the work of former generations—yes, we should always remember about their work with profound gratitude, for it was very exhausting and self-sacrificing toil. First of all, men studied the languages of the ancient peoples in their grammatical and lexicographical composition more carefully and fully than any other language in the world. The result of their labours was the profusely illustrated handbooks and dictionaries—not those, of course, which are familiar to you in your school course, but enormous volumes, the material for which was drawn from the whole sphere of ancient literature. It will be enough to mention that the "Thesaurus linguæ Græcæ" of Stephanus, that is to say, Etienne, the French scholar of the seventeenth century, comprises in the new edition nine supplementary volumes in folio, and that the corresponding "Thesaurus linguæ Latinæ," in the preparation of which almost all classical Germany is at the present moment engaged, promises to be still more imposing. So thus we are able, by studying the history of any word, to penetrate to the very soul of Antiquity—language, as you remember, is the confession of a people.

But this picture, perhaps, is not very attractive for you. Well, at any rate, let us be content that the work in this connection has been, to a considerable extent, already done. Another very important branch of this labour was the publication of explanatory editions of the classical authors—again, not those which you know, but of another kind, the aim of which was to connect together by a chain or net of ideas all the records of ancient literature with copious references to the corresponding records of archæology and the other aspects of classical learning. Thanks to that labour I have to possess but one piece of evidence to acquire immediately all the others—and how far that convenience in the finding of material lightens scientific study you can easily imagine. A third branch of the work was the compilation of dry, but very comprehensive, guides in the various departments of classical learning—political history, the history of literature, mythology, law, state administration, and so on, with the citation of all the evidence afforded not merely by literature but also by inscriptions and the other kinds of records.

All these subjects, then, taken together constitute that foundation of which I spoke, and on which we are only now beginning to build the fabric of our knowledge. Of course, the foundation itself is not yet quite complete. Fresh discoveries are constantly adding to and strengthening it, and this will be so for a long time to come. None the less, it is now sufficiently firm to support a substantial building. And what sort of a building that will be you will easily understand, if I tell you that as yet we have no history of ancient religion, nor even of mythology in its development, no history of ancient morality and mental outlook on things, no history of the intellectual, of the ordinary, or even of the material civilisation of the ancient peoples, no intelligent history of the ancient literatures, no history of economic and social phenomena even in their main factors, such as property or capitalism, and so on: if I tell you that the famous scholar Ihehring was occupied in the last days of his life by the idea of a history of Roman law, which he proposed to make a reference book not only for the jurist, but for every educated man—an idea which has to this day remained unrealised. . . .

For every educated man. Yes, classical learning indeed is a science to which the whole educated world turns without distinction of special occupations. But it also stands in what is known as mutualistic relations with that world. It borrows from the whole sphere of knowledge. Our opponents keep harping on its lack of self-sufficiency and count that as a ground for reproach. In my opinion, however, that expression is a term of the highest eulogy. Yes, our branch of science is not self-sufficient. At every turn we are forced to appeal for advice and evidence to the representatives of the other departments of knowledge, even in the comparatively narrow region of school classical reading, as I explained to you in my fourth lecture. This is because the science dealing with the ancient world deals with the world. It unites all branches of knowledge on the basis of phenomena, just as philosophy unites them on the ground of principles. The mathematician, the student of chemistry, and even of language, can pass his whole time within closed doors, within the four walls which enclose the special subject of his study. The classical scholar cannot do so, if only he wishes to be a learned man and not a mere craftsman. And the result of this constant intercourse with other sciences is a broad outlook on things, a consciousness of the unity of knowledge and a respect towards its different branches.

However, you know that already. It is now time to answer another question which you may raise. I mentioned a whole series of problems awaiting the classical scholarship of our times and the near future, the history of ancient religion, of intellectual culture, and so on. Well, and when you solve these problems—you may ask—what will you do then? When that times comes I believe that it will itself present new problems, about which speculation at the present moment is mere waste of time. Even those tasks which I have just mentioned were not dreamt of a hundred years ago. But one task will always remain for us, as it has remained up to this time—the duty of utilising the treasures of Antiquity to suit the needs of the age, the duty of mediation between our world and the ancient world. It is not for ourselves that we work and not for our own branch of knowledge only. Our science has no ground for existence, no right to exist, outside of mankind by whom and for whom it is being built up. We work for you, for your contemporaries and descendants —in a word, for society.

Even then, you ask, supposing society does not want to know you or your work ? Yes, gentlemen, even then. And yet, whether that supposition be true, and as far as it is true why and for what reason it should be so—about all that I must say a few words in the following lecture, which is the last.

LECTURE VIII

OUR talks have come back to the point whence they started. We began by formulating the fundamental difference that lies between the view of the world at large regarding the value of a classical training for education, for culture, and as a science—between that view and the opinion of the persons aware of the true facts of the case. Then I gave you to understand that this view of society, in so far as it is expressed in a conscious contempt for Antiquity, cannot compare for authority with that unconscious respect which precisely the same society has paid to it, and which has preserved its influence over the world during these many centuries after the fall of the ancient world itself.

Let us grant that this attitude of conscious contempt is not characteristic of all modern society. Still, it is a fact as regards a considerable part of it, and as such it requires an explanation. This also I gave you at the outset of my lectures. We can analyse, I said, the meaning of the hostility shown towards classical education ; we can distinguish the part played in it by well-meaning involuntary delusion from that which betrays conscious deception. I began, however, not with this negative, but with the positive aspect of our subject. I showed you what constitutes the importance of a classical training for education, for culture, and as a science. If Logos was gracious to you and to myself, if the task of persuasion which brought us hither has not proved a failure, then you know now that the opinion of the minority is the correct view, and that consequently the attitude of the majority, which is at variance with it, can only be explained as due to misunderstanding or deception. However, to leave no room for doubt, I shall bring you independent evidence for the negative part of my subject as well. And therewith I shall consider my task accomplished.

Either deception or misunderstanding. . . . Now in reality both the one and the other are equally contrary to that feeling for truth which a classical training implants in us. You remember that it makes not one but two demands of us; firstly, *do not lie,* and secondly, *do not be mistaken*—in those cases, of course, where it is possible not to be mistaken, where there are people and data to direct us to the path of truth. The moral signification, however, of these two sins against truth is different. It is a pleasure to point out the proper path to the victim of a mistake, but it is no pleasure, very far from a pleasure, to expose the methods of deceit. Let me begin with the second distasteful part of my subject to be the sooner rid of it.

First of all we must remember that these methods are not the original cause of that hostility of which

I speak—on the contrary, they necessarily presuppose it. Deception would have found no credence and so would have failed of its purpose, had it not fallen on hearts already prepared to receive it. This consideration, however, not only does not justify it, but is far from proving it harmless. Misunderstanding creates only a thin haze of uncertainty which the shafts of truth could still penetrate. But the dense fog of conscious deception thickens it and converts it at last into that impenetrable darkness which chokes us and drives us to despair. The history of all popular movements is full of examples of this principle. To begin with, some person or institution or idea falls from popularity, sometimes deservedly, sometimes not. Individuals come forward directly as popular leaders, and to heighten their influence pile up all manner of fictitious scandals about the object of popular dislike. Their method the Romans called *crescere ex aliquo*. Such calumnies are sure to meet with success. Every kind of nonsense wins credence, the calumniator becomes a universal favourite, and woe to that foolish zealot for truth who should conceive the idea of refuting him.

But, you will ask, where do I find deception and deceivers in the case under consideration ? There, I answer, where self-elected guides of popular opinion step forth on the scene in the columns of newspapers, the pages of magazines, and modern journalism generally. But how can we trace them there ? By collecting all the lies and slanders diffused through all Russia in our journalistic organs? That is not enough. We must expose the methods of deception. We must show how it in one case ignores facts, in another wilfully distorts them, in a third juggles and cheats with them like the veriest card-sharper. . . . But, gentlemen, where can we find time for all that? And yet I must direct your attention to this campaign of fraud, for I wish to inspire you with a sagacious suspicion of these evil-intentioned guides of your opinion. Fortunately there is another path available, which is shorter and not less conclusive. I shall indicate a case of deception in a quarter where least of all you would expect it by all internal and external conditions, and then I shall leave it to you to make the following deduction: "If they do these things in a green tree, what shall be done in the dry?" You will understand that under these circumstances my words imply as much respect to the person, whom I shall name, as reproach, for by citing him preferably to others I own him to be the green tree. And now allow me to read you the passage which I have in view. Here it is. The author is referring to classical examinations:

"And yet all these thick note-books have to be crammed and known in every trifling detail. For example, the subject discussed is some literary work of the ancient world, and in the course of the lecture two or three closely written pages are devoted to showing under whose editorship, in what year and place—Venice, Amsterdam, Rome, Paris—that work has been published during the course of two thousand (*sic*) years. All this it is absolutely necessary to know. Should the student make a mistake in the year of publication or in the editor's name, the professor throws up his hands in horror :

" 'Preserve us ! What do you mean ? Now, how without knowing that can you consider yourself an educated man ?'

" Is it surprising under such circumstances that our young men are generally so shockingly backward ?" And so on.

I have taken this passage from a book which enjoyed a wide circulation, and three editions of which ran out in a short period—the year 1903. Its title is " The School and Life," and its author Father G. S. Petroff. What is one to say about it ?

Well, first of all, I think that it would have been fitting for a man who writes and publishes books to have known in what year, or, if he is so averse to precise data, then roughly in about what century, the art of printing was invented, and not to have spoken about editions of the ancient authors published in Venice and Amsterdam with the date of their appearance and the name of the editor for these two thousand years. But that point is not vital for us. The author is discussing, as I said, classical examinations. He does not give the source of his evidence, but no matter—I am justified in saying that no one here in Petersburg is more conversant with these subjects than I am. Not only do I hold these examinations in our

Petersburg University, but for the last ten or twelve years I have been every year president of the Classical Board of Examiners in one or other of the provincial universities. Permit me, then, to assert, on the ground of that fairly wide experience, that Father Petroff's description of classical examinations is the purest invention without any likeness, even external, to reality. No examinations are held in Russia in the way he represents. Of course, lists of the editions of an author are to be found in the so-called *Bibliothecæ Scriptorum*—though, as you may guess, not for two thousand years, but for four hundred and a little more. That is exceedingly useful material for the information of classical scholars like myself, but not one of us would dream of driving that material into our own heads, much less of asking it from our students. I must admit, too, that there are answers given at examinations which make the professors hold up their hands in horror, but they are never about the year or place of an edition or an author. And yet, unfortunately, it is certain that such absurdities as the one which I have instanced are not only morally reprehensible but also practically harmful. Not long ago one of the students whom I was questioning in my capacity as chairman of the examining board complained to me that absolutely similar fabrications had caused him to waste a year of his life. He was a classic by inclination, but he could not bring himself to inscribe his name in the Classical Faculty, because in the provincial town where he had finished his school education he was told that the only work done in that Faculty was Greek and Latin composition. He embraced medicine, and a whole year passed before he returned to his favourite study, convinced at last by observing the occupations of the classical undergraduates that these stories were untrue. And who knows? Perhaps at this very moment some young man or other in the provinces, reading Father Petroff's book about the charms of classical examinations, and not suspicious of any fraud, is making a vow that nothing shall induce him to enter the Classical Faculty despite his abilities and taste for that branch of study, with the result that he may be beaten out of his line not for one year, but for all his life.

Of course, gentlemen, you understand that my instance is only a sample, only a small glass of the enormous bucket of slander with which we are deluged in modern journalism. My instance is interesting in the first place because its label bears a well-known and respected name, and secondly, because here the slander, if I may use the expression, is taken *in flagrante delicto*. It is not so easy in all cases. But still, I beg you to remember one thing. When you read in the newspapers or elsewhere a condemnation of classical study as a science and as a force for education and culture, then be sure that this is an attempt to deceive you. This warning should be borne in mind, especially when the author has not the courage to sign his name and takes cowardly shelter behind an anonymous or false signature. You will also understand, I hope, that personally I have nothing against Father Petroff, who, indeed, is far more after my heart than his enemies. On the contrary, I respect his missionary enterprise and wish him success in it. Let him sow the seeds of good and truth, let him teach people to observe the ten commandments, but let him observe them himself also—all of them, not excluding the ninth.

Let us now dismiss the question of deception and proceed to consider the second less objectionable source of popular hostility against the classics, namely, misunderstanding. In regard to this point we should distinguish between the classical world as an object of education and as a force for culture. The third division of our subject, namely, the value of classical study as a science, does not call for mention in this connection. Of course, this third aspect also suffers from the nonsense propagated abroad, and especially in print. To speak seriously, however, not a single thinking man questions but that a science dealing with the classics has as much right to exist as Sanskritology, Egyptology, or other equally inoffensive branches of knowledge. Moreover, the second aspect also may be dismissed. Our motto, "Not a model, but a seed," sufficiently indicates where the misunderstanding lies on this score. We shall deal, therefore, only with the first aspect, namely, the prejudice against a classical education in schools. Both in Russia and in Western Europe it is reproached with two offences.

Firstly, it is unnecessary; secondly, it is difficult. These two charges, which are common to Russia and Europe, are augmented with us by a third, which constitutes our national peculiarity. Classical education, please remark, is retrograde! This is the point to which the catch-words refer—classical obscurantism, classical "muzzles," and so on. We shall reserve this consideration for later on: to work time, to amusement an hour.

And as *work* in this connection let us consider the first reproach, namely, that classical education in schools is unnecessary. I have mentioned it here, of course, not to refute it. Why it is necessary I have already tried to explain to you, as far as time allowed, in my first four lectures. My task now is a different one. I must analyse public opinion and show you how a prejudice against classics could and must have arisen. And the reasons are quite clear. In estimating the value of a branch of knowledge a man inexperienced in the work in question is apt to adopt a narrow utilitarian point of view and make its value dependent on its immediate applicability to life and practical work. Let us take a ready-made dress as an example. Every savage will understand that a dress is a useful thing, protecting one as it does from heat and cold. Now show that savage a sewing machine. He will merely wave his arms, not understanding what is the use of such a thing. But it may be shown to him, by illustration, that it is this machine which makes the dress, and he will now, though without understanding anything, admit its use. But then these sewing machines, in their turn, are made somehow or other. Special factories exist for this purpose and turn out, with a deafening din of machinery, rods, pinions, screws, nuts, and so on. Take any of these factory machines, and a man without technical education will not understand in the least what is the use of it. It is the same with classical education. The mental work immediately useful for the world is produced by the mind—that is our sewing machine. But the mind also must be produced somehow or other and adapted for useful work. One of the machines which produce it is our classical education in schools. This fact, however, can be understood only by a man who possesses the corresponding technical knowledge. A man without that knowledge will always be inclined to admit that instruction in the classics is a useless waste of time and labour.

And labour. . . . Yes, and that word brings us to the second reproach levelled at classical education in schools. Here the misunderstanding obviously does not consist in the fact itself—classical work in schools is difficult if pursued conscientiously—there is no need of discussing the point. The misunderstanding lies in the deduction, which is drawn from that fact. It is difficult, people say, and so away with it! It is difficult, I rejoin, and that is an extra reason for keeping it. I ask you, gentlemen, to pay special attention to this point. Now more than ever I shall be forced to lean upon the thinker's code of honour. I shall have to warn you against being carried away by one very honourable and amiable feeling, namely, the sentiment of humanity. I have been long conscious of one retort with which you might meet all that I said to you in my first lectures. I may express it thus: "There were fifty of us when we entered the first class, and there are only thirty of us left to pass out.* The others found the course beyond their powers, and for the greater part of them the stumbling-block was the ancient languages." Hence one can understand their animosity against classical study—their own, their parents' and relatives', and yours also through the feelings of comradeship.

That reproach against classical education I could very easily overlook. When the Commission for the Reform of Secondary Schools, to which I alluded before, was discussing the subject of the failures, certain members, who had investigated that question with care, brought forward statistics for both the principal types of secondary schools. The percentage of failures in the classical schools proved to be exactly the same as in the modern schools, namely forty per cent. That one fact by itself shows that it is not the classical languages which are responsible for the failures, but something else, which is common to both types of

* The Leaving Certificate of the Russian schools, now accepted at Cambridge as an equivalent for the Preliminary Examination, is important in connection with military and other services, entrance to the universities, and so on.

secondary schools. What that something is I can tell you now. It is the law of selection. But then, when the question was debated by the Commission, opinions set in another direction. The majority of the members became a mouthpiece for popular animosity against a school guilty of producing failures. I remember well the outburst of magnanimous enthusiasm with which a gentleman actively interested in the question of secondary schools and celebrated for his humanitarian feelings announced: "If a school takes in a hundred pupils, it should also pass out a hundred pupils." So, I said to myself, entrance guarantees the receipt of a certificate. Well, and what guarantees entrance? The only possible answer is, influence or bribery. . . . But that is a point to which we shall return later.

I do not wish to pass over the reproach as to the difficulty of classical school work. I said before that its difficulty is an extra recommendation. I ask you to fix your attention on what I may call the sociological significance of the school. This is its scheme in brief.

The organisation of our society is, of course, still very far from being complete. One of the principal reasons why it is so imperfect is the fact that there are in it still too many drones—that is to say, people who are capable of work, but prefer to live at the expense of others. We doom that type, however, to utter extinction; we ask that every farthing in the citizen's pocket should be a farthing gained by his own work.

According to our ideal society is an army of work. Now every army has its common soldiers and officers, its lower and higher ranks. The boundary between the two is not specially sharp even in the regular military army, and in the army of work there is no definite line of demarcation at all. But still, even in this latter army, distinctions may be and should be made between the apex and the base of the social pyramid. Who, then, are its officers? Obviously not government officials only, but every one who commands rather than obeys, who serves society with intellectual rather than physical work, and that, too, intellectual work of greater and not less value, managers and foremen of factories, directors of commercial enterprises, landowners, or inspectors of field labour, doctors, artists, and so on. In different periods, one should note, however, the composition of that élite of society has varied. Under normal conditions they enjoy a large salary in comparison with the common soldiers; they live in clean, bright homes and not in kennels, corners, and night-shelters. How, then, are people appointed to be officers? That is the point which constitutes the different character of the various periods. The criterion which distinguished the candidate for an officer's post from the candidate for a common soldier's duties has always been a valuation, only the character of the valuation has varied at various times. In primitive ages it was doubtless rude physical strength. In civilised epochs we see first of all the principle of birth; the place at the apex of the social pyramid falls hereditarily from noble father to noble son. Then the valuation by birth was replaced by a valuation by property, or crossed with it. At the present time the valuation is chiefly by education, and it is obvious that this system will obtain in the future. Who, then, are the candidates for officers' posts in the army of work? You yourselves, gentlemen, who are finishing your education in the secondary schools.

I should now like to summon a vision before you, an ominous, imposing, and alas! exceedingly real vision. It is a young man of your years, only he is dressed not in clean clothes, but filthy, evil-smelling rags. On his head he wears not a smart cap like yours, but a workman's greasy hat. His face bears the marks of the privation and the vice which haunt the lives of those "at the bottom" of the social pyramid.* You introduce yourselves to each other. "I," you say, "by the grace of God, am a candidate for an officer's post." "And I," your vision answers, "by the wrath of God, am of the proletariate." And fixing a vicious glance on you he asks: "And why is it, sir, you become an officer and I not?" Two answers are possible to this question, the first a very disgraceful one, the second a very good one. The former is: "Because my father was a man comparatively well to do, who paid for my education in a secon-

* A reference to a drama by Maxim Gorki, in which the characters are taken from the dregs of the community. The common expression for these outcasts in Russia nowadays is "the Gorki type."

dary school seven or eight years in succession, and during that time gave me leisure for my studies, whereas your father, supposing you had a father, was a poor devil, who fed and brought you up on copper farthings and at the same time exploited your labour." Yes, that answer will, unfortunately, contain a large proportion of truth; but I fancy the conscience in each one of you will shrink from it. The second answer, against which no reproach is possible, is: "Because I have gone through an amount of mental work which would be beyond your power. Only think, fifty of us entered the first class and only thirty pass out."

And now let me ask you—which of these two answers is more in harmony with the idea of the easy school, the school that passes out as many pupils as it received? Obviously not the second answer, but the first, an answer which you would not bring yourself to utter—your tongue would refuse its office. Now just imagine that this idea of an easy school were realised. The inscription "Industry and Ability" is torn down once for all from the school door and replaced by the device: "We ask your favour! A certificate guaranteed to all." What will be the result? Yes, we ask your favour! A school has accommodation for only fifty, and the number of applications is five hundred. Or do you think there will not be so many? Why, even at present, when the difficulty of the course deters many, the number of those who wish to enter is twice or three times greater than the number of vacancies. And what will happen when the ease of the course and the certainty of a .certificate form additional attractions? Every father, as you may guess, wishes to see his son an officer. No, indeed, not less than five hundred. Well, how are we to choose the fifty happy individuals out of that number? One method is to raise the school fee proportionately, that is to say, establish on a legal and lasting footing just that system of valuation by property which is the meanest and most pernicious of all the criteria, and allow it also as a culminating point of meanness to screen itself under the mask of the criterion of education. Another means is a severe entrance examination. That would involve the changing of the time of struggle and failure from the schoolboy's to the child's age. Such a method flies in the face of Nature and is opposed to common sense. An easy youth following a hard and exhausting childhood! No, of course, neither the one nor the other are suitable. A third will be applied, and this one all the more because it has in Russia a very valid historical and actual foundation. That means is protection or bribery. It also will be a kind of selection, not, however, natural selection, tending to improvement, but corrupt selection, resulting in degeneration. However, it will not enjoy a long triumph. That vision, which I summoned before you, and whose existence should not be forgotten, will not tolerate that abuse. The history of the eighteenth century in France is significant. If a privileged class thinks of annulling or lightening that amount of work which alone justifies its privileges, then it will be swept away by a revolution. For heaven's sake do not ask for, do not introduce, an easy school! An easy school is a crime against society.

And that is why, however painful it may be, I warn you against being carried away by feelings of humanity and sympathy with your comrades who have failed. That humanitarian sentiment is but the short-sighted bourgeois instinct of a caste. You are sorry for your companions who entered school with you and who, in consequence of a lack of industry or ability, do not pass out with you. I, too, am sorry for them, but I am much more sorry for those contemporaries of yours who, notwithstanding their application to study and their capabilities, were debarred by external circumstances from crossing the threshold of a secondary school. Their failure is a far more melancholy phenomenon than the failure of the former, since society itself suffers from it, whereas the only people to suffer from your companions' failures are your companions themselves. The failure of the capable is a drag on progress, the failure of the incapable an instrument of progress.

That is why the ideal school organisation will be a position of affairs in which the failure of industrious and able scholars will be impossible, even though this should necessitate an increase in the percentage of failures of the supine and incapable. That idea will be realised, as generally speaking every ideal is realised, by means of the two powerful levers of progress, differentiation and unification. Differentiation demands the greatest possible diversity of types of secondary schools. We have classical schools, modern schools, professional schools of various kinds. Excellent. The more of these types, the greater amount of chances that every capable boy finds the one to suit his abilities. Unification demands the union of all types of primary, secondary, and most advanced schools into one organism, a kind of majestic tree. The roots of that tree will be the primary town and country schools. Reaching deep down among the people, they should seek out individuals capable of intellectual work and raise them, according to their abilities, to the trunk, the branches, the top of the tree. Such a school will be a really popular one, that is to say, in the poet's idea, " one that breaks in so many good men of the people "—an expression which cannot be applied as yet to our present schools, and which can never be applied to the easy school which some people project. An easy school is an institution for effeminate sprigs of gentle birth, a monstrous and humiliating revival of the serfdom system on a capitalistic basis.

And when we attain to that ideal which I pictured, then the question of the failures will be solved in a way which, if not fully satisfactory to us, is yet the normal answer. You don't succeed in the classical school ? Well, try your luck in the modern. You can't stand the modern ? Go over to the classical. You don't find the place suited for you in either the one or the other ? Then choose a technical school, according to your inclination. In this search you may waste a year or two of your life. Well, what can be done ? Reproach yourself or your parents for not having found you straight off the school suited for you ! Or perhaps there is no such school at all ? You are unfitted for intellectual work ? Well, take up some trade ! Go as a cabin-boy on board ship, or return to mother earth. If you can't be an officer, be a private in the army of work. You are unfit for physical work also ? You are weak, delicate, disabled ? . . . or perhaps insuperably lazy and slothful ? Then, poor fellow—it is terrible for me to say what then, but you understand yourself what the law of selection answers for me : "Then —die. . . ."

Should we, can we acquiesce in that law ?

Gentlemen, we have touched here on a very important question. But we have very little time left, and we must still consider the third charge against classical education, namely that it is retrograde. Perhaps, however, you will release me from the necessity of entering minutely upon that point and proving to you that the study of Antiquity, the source of all the ideas of freedom on which our civilisation lives, cannot in any way be called retrograde. I think, indeed, that this fact has been already sufficiently brought out in my former lectures. Did they imply many retrograde elements ? But, you ask, how could such an opinion originate ? First of all, I imagine, some government official, who did not see the world from behind his green table, might conceive the bright idea that perfects and supines could be used as a counterpoise to the revolutionary inclinations of society. This recalls the Middle Ages, when the right of science to exist depended on its influence upon morality and religion, and it was set down to the credit of arithmetic that it distracted men's minds from sinful thoughts. This project frightened an army of officious journalists for the liberalism of their future readers, and they proceeded to lay the blame for the idea on classical learning itself, which was perfectly innocent. Which of these parties was the wiser, I do not know. But Cicero was perhaps right when he said in a similar case : " If, as a well-known proverb asserts, the wisest man is he who can devise what is necessary, and the second wisest man he who follows the wise counsels of his neighbour, then it is quite the reverse in regard to the opposite quality ; the man who cannot devise a sensible plan is less foolish than he who approves of another's foolish plan." And that it is precisely this opposite quality with which we are now concerned is easily seen from the fact that this charge of a retrograde tendency is brought against classical education in Russia only. Had perfects and supines really possessed that miraculous force for conservatism, which the wooden psychology of these gentlemen has in view, then, I fancy, the sharp-witted West would scarce have left them the honour of the discovery.

And now allow me to put all that nonsense

aside and return to the interesting and important question on which I touched a moment ago.

We were speaking of the sociological signification of the secondary school in general and the classical school in particular. That signification consists, as we saw, in the selection of "candidates for the posts of officers in the army of work"; that is to say, the selection of individuals capable of intellectual work from the number of all those summoned or willing to serve. For that purpose a school ought to be more or less difficult. An easy school presupposes easy work—and that invention must be left to the inventor of cold fire and hot snow. Work, as far as it is work, must always be difficult.* I have been attacked for this sociological rôle which my opponents charge me of foisting upon schools. So, according to you, they ask, a school ought to be a kind of sieve? Now I have nothing against people inclined to idle jokes picturing my school under the symbol of a sieve. I would only ask them to raise that conception of a sieve to the level of the usual symbols used for representing Life and Nature. Wherever only life is, a struggle for it goes on, in the course of which the fit survive and the unfit die out. If a school wishes to preserve its life, it must not seek to evade the law that governs life in general. But I protest against the idea that I am foisting this rôle on a school as one which it should perform consciously and directly. No, gentlemen! That idea is founded on a misconception of that heterogeneity

* There is a play of words in the Russian.

of purposes, which I mentioned in my first lecture. This principle is manifested everywhere, where the law of selection is at work, and consists, as you remember, in the non-correspondence of the conscious and immediate purpose with the unconscious and indirect purpose. Consciously and immediately the school should aim at but one object, the education of its pupils. It need not even dream of any other. But just by this process of bringing its pupils to a certain level of education, and also presumably letting those go for whom that level is unattainable—just by this process it serves also unconsciously the purpose of selection. And woe to it if it should become conscious of that involuntary indirect mission which it serves and dream of evading that duty and altering its direct educative purpose accordingly! Such a school would be swept off the scene once for all by another school viewing its duties more seriously. Yes, we have before us a sharp but inevitable choice of alternatives. A school must be either an instrument of progress or its victim.

But what, then, are we to do with our "failure"? We have tried to settle him in schools of various kinds and put him at last to physical work. Everywhere he has proved incapable. Well, are we to subscribe to the stern command of the law of selection—the command "Die!"?

No! That law needs to be supplemented. Of course, a struggle for existence rules over all the sphere of life; so too its consequence, namely, the survival of the fit, or natural selection. In mankind alone that law crosses with another important and powerful principle—the principle of love. This principle is not, of course, an exception—exceptions are inadmissible in the law of selection—but its highest possible development. Love came down on the earth not to break that law but to complete it. The law of selection leads mankind to improvement. But improvement is not only physical and intellectual, it is moral as well. When a rod vibrating with continuous acceleration of movement attains a certain degree of rapidity, a new force is originated, and the rod begins to shine. It is the same with humanity when it reaches a certain degree of progress in civilisation. Something new and marvellous is kindled in it, namely, the moral law, which bids a man love his neighbour, and instead of pushing over a falling fellow-creature, so as to have more room for himself, stretch out a helping hand and share his own possessions with him. Primitive society may kill off its old men who are unfit for physical work and an extra burden; it obeys but one law—the law of the struggle for existence. We, however, members of civilised society, share with our old men the bread won by our toil because we love them. Now suppose some one says to us: "Why do you do that? Whatever is falling should be pushed over in view of still greater physical and intellectual progress. Acting otherwise you condemn yourselves to degeneration." What is our answer? "No," we say; "we do not wish a physical and mental progress which is purchased at the price of moral deterioration." The same principle marks our treatment of our failures. We do not annihilate them, we care for them. We build hospitals for the failures of physical life—the sick, asylums for the failures of intellectual life—idiots and lunatics, prisons for the failures of moral life—criminals. We try to make their lives there endurable. So within the principal part of our society, which lives on the work system, there is vegetating a more or less considerable amount of people who do not share in the common work, people whose existence is justified and made normal by what I may call the "charity" system. These form the camp-followers of the army of work. We share our gains with them, but nothing more. We cannot permit the life juices of the healthy organisms capable of work to pass to the failures. That would indeed lead to the degeneration with which some people threaten us. We ought to tack more or less skilfully between two degenerations—on the one hand, moral degeneration, due to excessive insistence on the law of the struggle for existence and neglect of the law of love; and on the other hand, physical and intellectual degeneration, due to excessive enthusiasm for this latter law.

We have now our answer ready. We do not subscribe to that stern condemnation "Die!" which the law of selection pronounced on our failure. We say to him: "Off with you to the camp-followers. There you will receive means for a more or less tolerable vegetation—but, of course, nothing more." There is not much comfort in this picture. But what can be done? For all our wishes we cannot do away with the dark aspects of our life. And it will be a good thing if we succeed in the more or less near future in realising that ideal of which I speak here, the ideal of school organisation, with the implied full application of the principles of differentiation and unification, with the securing for all capable and industrious persons a place corresponding to their merits in the army of work. That will be an enormous progress in comparison with what has been and what is.

Progress. Yes, that word is the real final note in that symphony of thoughts and feelings which I wished to awaken in you. Progress is the watchword of that civilisation which is rooted in Antiquity. Towards it conduces all the play of those ideas which Antiquity has bequeathed to us, or in whose direction it has urged us during these fifteen hundred years of united life with it. Progress, too, is the object of the school which has classical education as its central point, not merely directly as a nursery of progressive ideas, but also indirectly as a means of sociological selection. For a long, a very long time, the West alone was the bearer of progressive ideas, the West which alone took over Antiquity to be the moving force of its civilisation. That was not what we had and have in the East—there we have a strange life, also civilised, but founded on the supposition that to-morrow must be exactly like to-day and yesterday. In comparison with the eternally thinking, eternally restless thought of the West, this majestic rest of the East is deeply impressive, this unconscious assurance that everything attainable has been attained, that to strive further is idle, foolish, sinful. Russia has been placed by history on the very border between East and West. Here both ideals conflict. Russia is the only one of the countries of European civilisation where the law of progress and its necessity have been disputed, the law of selection and its purpose disputed, the value of science and art disputed, the only country where the nervous question: "But that surely leads to degeneration and death?" has been followed by the quietly majestic answer: "Well, we must just degenerate and die!" Against that point of view I am powerless. All my arguments in favour of classical education were founded on a faith in progress, in its possibility and necessity. If you decide to deny progress, then all that I have said is overthrown.

Well, are we to begin a fresh discussion on this new, all-embracing theme? No, we must stop some time or other. Every thought, when followed out to its conclusion, raises a whole chain of new thoughts. If this happen here also with you, it will be only good for you. I have invited you to see in Antiquity not a model but a seed. Clearly, then, I cannot ask more for my own lectures about Antiquity. Let them also be a seed of thought for you. I hope that if not now, then, at any rate, some time or other, this seed will sprout in you and give forth fruit. Perhaps then you will have forgotten the subject of these talks of ours and will rejoice at the crop which has sprung up in you under the belief that it is actually your own—and you will be right. Whatever a man has worked up in himself or worked out of himself is his own. It cannot be taken from him, and there is nothing else which a man can call his own mental property. But still, I should not like to close on a question mark. As you, however, are exhausted and I am exhausted myself, I shall follow the example of my favourite author, Plato, and conclude my discourse on the theme, upon which I have just touched, with an allegory. So here you have my parable about progress—as a kind of parting salutation and souvenir of what I trust were pleasant hours.

When the angels had fallen and their evil and insolent devices brought on them a merited punishment, two of the fallen, Orientius and Occidentius, were deemed worthy of pardon as being less guilty. They were not cast away for ever. They were permitted to redeem their sin by a laborious task, that with its completion they might return to the cloisters of heaven. The task consisted of this—to go on foot, with a staff in the hand, a journey of many million miles. When this sentence was pronounced on them, the elder of the twain, Orientius, besought the Creator and said: "O Lord, show me yet one mercy! Grant that my path should be straight and even, that there be no hills and dales to delay me, that I see before me the final goal towards which I journey!" And the Creator said to him: "Your prayer shall be fulfilled." And he turned to the other and asked: "And you, Occidentius, do you desire nothing?" And he answered: "Nothing." With that they were let go. Then a mist of oblivion enwrapped them, and when they came to themselves, they awoke each one on that place which was the destined starting-point of their journey.

Orientius stood up and looked round him. A staff lay close by. All around stretched out, like a sea asleep, an immeasurable flat unbroken plain, over it the blue sky, boundless and cloudless everywhere; only in one place far away at the very edge of the horizon shone a white light. He understood that there was the place whither he should direct his steps. He grasped his staff and went forward. He journeyed on for a day or two and then gazed all round him again, and it seemed to him that the distance which separated him from his goal had not decreased by a single step, that he was still ever standing in the same place and still ever surrounded by the same immeasurable plain as before. "No," he said in despair, "eternity is too short to cross a space like this." And with these words he flung away his staff, sank down hopelessly on the ground, and fell asleep. He slept for a long time, right up to our own age.

At the same time as his elder brother, Occidentius also awoke. He rose up and looked round him. Behind him was the sea, in front a hollow, beyond the hollow a wood, beyond the wood a hill, and a white light seemed to be burning on the hill. "Is that all!" he exclaimed gaily. "I shall be there by evening." He grasped a staff that lay by his feet and set out on his journey. And indeed before evening he had reached the top of the hill, but there he saw that he had been mistaken. Only from the distance it had appeared that the light was burning on the hill; in reality there was nothing on it save some apple trees, with whose fruits he allayed his hunger and thirst. On the other side was a descent, and below ran a river. Over the river a hill rose, and on the hill shone ever the same white light. "Well, what?" said Occidentius. "I shall rest, and after that to the road! In two days I shall be there, and then straight into heaven!" Again his calculation proved right, but again it was not heaven that he found. Behind the hill was a new, broad valley, beyond the valley rose a higher hill, whose top was crowned by the rays of the white light. Of course, our pilgrim felt a certain vexation, but not for long. The hill beckoned him irresistibly forward; there at last for sure were the gates of heaven! And so ever on and on, day after day, week after week, month after month, year after year, age after age. Hope is succeeded by disillusion, from disillusion rises a fresh hope. He is moving forward at this very moment. Ravines, rivers, crags, impassable bogs delay his progress. Many times he has wandered off the path and lost the guiding light; he has made circuitous marches and turned back till he has succeeded in marking again the reflection of the longed-for brightness. And now boldly, with his trusty staff in his hand, he is climbing up a high hill, the name of which is "The Social Problem." The hill is steep and craggy. He must struggle through many ravines and thickets and scale abrupt walls and precipices, but he does not despair. Before him he sees the gleam of the light, and he is firmly assured that he has but to win the summit, and the gates of heaven will open before him.

THE END

APPENDIX

Russian Writers and Painters

Dostoyevski.—Born in Moscow in October, 1821. When twenty-four years of age he wrote his "Poor People," and sprang immediately into fame. In 1849 he was condemned to death on political grounds, and with his companions was already on the scaffold when a messenger came from Nicolas I with a reprieve. Transported to Siberia, he was detained for four years in prison in Omsk, and then made a soldier. He was pardoned in 1859 after the accession of Alexander II. He died in January, 1881. His works are written hurriedly and carelessly, but show remarkable genius, an intimate knowledge of psychology, and profound philosophical thought. He is, perhaps, the greatest of all Russian writers. His best-known novel in Western Europe is "Crime and Punishment." "The Brothers Karamazoff," his greatest work, and the novel generally called "Devils"—a more proper title would be "Unclean Spirits"—along with a large amount of minor work, have not yet been translated into English.

LIESKOFF.—The "Kolivanski mujz" was published about forty years ago. In some respects Lieskoff is the precursor of Tchekhoff and Gorki. He wrote chiefly short stories. His best-known work is probably the masterly sketch "Nowhither."

NEKRASOFF (1821–1877).—The son of an army officer. As a student he spent a wretched life, but by sheer energy eventually became owner of "The Contemporary." The subject of his poetry is the life of the Russian masses in town and country. It is marked by sincerity and a real sympathy with the lower classes. The style lacks ease and spontaneity, and an exaggerated political bias constantly obtrudes itself. He is a poet with a purpose; he himself called his muse "the muse of vengeance and misery." Exalted at his death by socialistic Russia over Pushkin and Lermontoff, he is now beginning to be forgotten. To unprejudiced readers he seems a much smaller figure.

PETROFF.—Father Petroff is a prominent figure in modern Russia. He was Professor of Theology in the Polytechnical Institute, a great college in Petersburg. His work among the poor and his preaching, flavoured with rationalism and radicalism—he interpreted the Lord's Prayer in a revolutionary sense—gave him wide influence among the capital populace, who returned him as member for the second Duma, but led him into difficulties with his ecclesiastical superiors. He was first confined for a term to a monastery, and later defrocked. On this occasion he sent an interesting document to the Metropolitan indicative of his beliefs, which appears in the (English) "Contemporary," March, 1908. He now lives in retirement in Finland.

POGODIN (1800–1875).—An historian and archæologist, born at Moscow and eventually professor in Moscow University. Besides historical studies and translations, he published works on Russian and Slavonic Antiquities; for this purpose he had travelled all over European Asia, the southern Slav countries, and Siberia. In Western Europe he is perhaps best known by his "Studies in the Chronicle of Nestor," translated into German by F. Lœwe, Petersburg, 1844.

PUSHKIN.—Born in Moscow in 1802, and killed in a duel, like Lermontoff, in 1857. One of the greatest poets of modern times. His chief works are the novels, "The Captain's Daughter" and "The Queen of Spades"; and in poetry, besides several volumes of short pieces, "Boris Godunoff," "Ruslan and Ludmilla," "Don Juan," and, above all, "Evgeniy Oniegin," from which are derived several quotations in the present work.

REPIN, an historical painter, born in 1844, is still alive. His pictures of Tolstoy are well known in this country. Other examples of his art, well represented in the Tretyakoff Gallery, Moscow, are "Ivan the Terrible," "The Cossacks Beyond the

Dneppr Rapids," "A Village Procession," "Sowing on the Volga."

SOLOVIOFF, VLADIMIR (1853–1900).—The son of a famous historian, a professor in Moscow University. He had a brilliant career as a student and lecturer in Moscow and Petersburg Universities. Soon after the murder of Alexander II, in 1881, he used some imprudent expressions in a public lecture, and he retired into literary work. He is a subtle and profound thinker deserving of study in this country. His chief works are "Philosophic Principles of Knowledge," "Criticism of Abstract Principles," "Lectures on the God-Man." The Tolstoyan position is combated (p. 123) in "Three Conversations," admirably written dialogues in Plato's manner, which one may venture to hope will be translated soon into English.

TOLSTOY, COUNT ALEKSAI KONSTANTINOVITCH (1817–1875).—Author of an historical novel, "Prince Serebryanyi," and three tragedies, "The Death of Ivan the Terrible," "The Tsar Feodor Ivanovitch," and "Boris Godunoff." He wrote also some excellent satiric and epigrammatic verse and a few poems, which have caught with great success the spirit of the ancient folk poetry.

TOLSTOY, COUNT LYOFF NICOLAIEVITCH.—Born at Yasnaya Polyana ("Bright Meadow"), in the Government of Tula, in 1828. Karateyeff is the religious peasant in "War and Peace," and Akim a character in "The Power of Darkness."

VASNIETSOFF, a painter, born in 1848 and still alive. His most famous secular picture is a fine study of Scythian horsemen crossing a virgin steppe; but he is best known for his religious work, as, for example, his ornamentation of the dome in the Church of St. Vladimir, Kieff.

VYAZEMSKI, PRINCE (1793-1878).—A *littérateur* and frequent contributor to "The Contemporary," the great review founded by Pushkin. His works fill twelve large volumes, and preserve the pseudo-classical, sentimental attitude which vanished generally before Pushkin's romanticism. He fought against the French in 1812. He was Associate-Minister of Education, and became a state councillor in 1855.

INDEX

I

II

III

DATE DUE

Printed in USA